MAKE WAY FOR LOVE
A Story to Open Your Heart

MAKE WAY FOR LOVE

A Story To Open Your Heart

Lency Spezzano, M.S.

PSYCHOLOGY
VISI*of*ON

Psychology of Vision®
Press

Make Way For Love
A Story to Open Your Heart

Portions from *A Course In Miracles* © 1975
by Foundation for Inner Peace, Inc.
PO Box 1104, Glen Ellen, CA 95442   USA
Used with permission. The ideas expressed herein include the author's
personal interpretation and understanding of some of the concepts
found in *A Course In Miracles* and are not necessarily endorsed by the
copyright holder of the *Course*.

Cover art: Bruce Harman

ISBN 0-9643435-0-9 (Soft cover)
ISBN 0-9643435-1-7 (Hard cover)

Library of Congress Catalog Card Number: 94-69093

Manufactured in the United States
10 9 8 7 6 5 4 3 2 1

Psychology of Vision® Press
47-416 Waihee Place
Kaneohe, HI 96744
USA

Make way for love, which you did not create, but which you can extend. On earth this means forgive your brother, that the darkness may be lifted from your mind. When light has come to him through your forgiveness, he will not forget his savior, leaving him unsaved. For it was in your face he saw the light that he would keep beside him, as he walks through darkness to the everlasting Light.

A Course In Miracles, Text, p. 568

To Chuck, my True Husband, my partner, and savior.

ACKNOWLEDGEMENTS

Firstly and with great pride, I acknowledge my husband, Chuck Spezzano, Ph.D., for his theory and methods (the Psychology of Vision®) which have found their way into my work, and reflect in the stories found in this book. At this point it is impossible to define where my ideas begin, and his leave off.

I thank Mark Wadleigh, my friend and partner in this project. For his vision of the book, his ideas and editing, including the countless hours of transcribing my material into his computer with two fingers, I am very grateful. Mark's chapter, "The Boys," along with his constant support and encouragement have been invaluable.

I thank Peggy Chang for her cheerful typing of the manuscript, Batyah Elizabeth of Elizabeth Publications for layout of the pre-publication manuscript, and Susan How for all her help. Special thanks to Ken Shaw for his assistance in publishing, and for putting the book into its final form.

I thank my children, Christopher and J'aime, for developing and maturing me, and my parents for modeling a successful love relationship.

For their contributions to my understanding and for giving me the opportunity for so much receiving, I thank my seminar and counseling clients throughout the years.

I acknowledge *A Course In Miracles* for the miracles and sanity it has brought to my life.

And finally, I must thank all of the children and families of The Young People's Support Center (now renamed "HUGS For Hawaii's Seriously Ill Children and Their Families.") You have been my loving and courageous Teachers.

Contents

INTRODUCTION

At age 28, it seemed as if I had it all–success, recognition, opportunities, attractiveness..."the good life." Good except one thing–I could not feel it. I could not feel much of anything. Things were not really bad, but they were never *really* good. Any happiness was fleeting and shallow. Disillusioned and dissatisfied, I was ashamed to admit even to myself that I could neither love nor feel loved. I knew I was missing the best part of life.

My awakening came out of the desire to be real, truly human and to know myself. Step by step, the school of life brought me into personal, mystical contact with Love. I learned how to allow Love's grace to flow out to others as a healing agent.

Today, at age forty, I can feel again, and love has become a tangible essence and force in my life. It sweetens, heals, strengthens and makes things right when things go wrong. It reaches into the hearts of those I join, washes away pain and sorrow, and initiates the capacity for intimacy and ecstasy.

This connection to the Source of Love is the pleasure for which the human heart is made, the purpose for which we are designed, and the joy for which we are created. It is what I wish for all of us.

This is not a "how to" book about learning to love, because we learn to love by being loved. You and I do not have the opportunity to sit together and share this experience. My hope is that through your relationship with this book, through the italicized sections which are written to speak directly to *you,* you can receive love that will touch your heart, open it to transformation, and start you on a quest for further growth.

As you read about the experiences that opened my heart, I hope that you will allow yourself to feel everything that stirs within you, feel everything you can–even deadness and dissociation, if they arise; it is all part of the process.

Once love has had its way with you, once it has forged a bond connecting you to others with unlimited and unconditional tenderness, the world will unfold in ways beyond your present imagining. Uncharted realms of bliss and oneness with all of life beckon. May this book be a step toward that Beauty, and a companion on your journey Home.

Hello Sweetheart. It is good that you have come. I have waited the longest time to speak with you, and it is only this way that I have known to reach you. And reach you I have...

You...
        Specifically...
             Personally...
                  You.

Now that you are here, there is so much that I want to tell you. So much to share. That which is learned the hard way over many years, I want you to discover with ease. I wish you had not forgotten all of this long ago. The important thing is that you can remember it now.

There is a secret beyond the first veil of perception. A secret that cannot usually be seen, that must be felt through an open heart, that unlocks the meaning of life, making the life we have known a mere illusion compared to the greater life that begs to be experienced.

Some have paid the greatest of prices to discover the secret. Those who have, have never regretted the cost. Some have even paid with their lives.

This is the story of just such a soul. I hope that through his simple message you will easily gain the prize that cost him his life to win....

ARTHUR

On the last day of Arthur's life, a gorgeous, tropical summer day in 1982, he gave me the gift of a lifetime. My story begins three months before.

He was 19 years old when his physician referred him to me. Arthur's mind had raised a massive defense against the awareness that he was dying of cancer, and nothing could reach him. The doctor's voice over the telephone asked quietly if our center could help.

He was a local boy of Filipino ancestry, from a small town about an hour's drive down coast on the island of Oahu, Hawaii. Unaccustomed to such a young cancer patient, Arthur's doctor was deeply attached to him, and wanted him to understand that he was dying. He wanted him to be able to make his peace with the world, and meet his death as consciously as possible.

Arthur had visited my agency's support program for kids with life-threatening illnesses. Although he had given a lot of support to others, he told no one there that he was sick. His denial sometimes caused him to refuse medical treatment at the hospital. When he was hospitalized, Arthur never let his family visit. Although I had spent time with Arthur, I had never really "reached" him.

Then one morning, the doctor phoned to tell me that Arthur had been admitted to the hospital again. He probably would not live out the day. Could I please try one last time to help him? As I drove there, I felt afraid that I would prove inadequate to the situation, that what I could do or say would not be enough.

It was an achingly beautiful, balmy day in Waikiki; the hospital looked out onto the beach and the slopes of Diamond Head. Arthur lay alone in a tiny, windowless room, hooked up by needles and tubes to a blood transfusion apparatus. Liver failure had caused his skin to turn the yellow color of a school bus, and there was a deathly sick look in his jaundiced eyes.

I sat beside him, and with all my heart I opened myself up to him as much as I could. I looked into his face, and, after a minute, asked him, "What's it like?" For the first time we really looked into each other's eyes. Then, with a tug we could feel in our hearts, it was as though a veil fell away, and for the first time intimacy sprang up between us.

He spoke directly to me, not through the usual tangle of fear and denial. With the voice of clarity and certainty, he told me what he had learned from life.

"I used to think I knew what was important. I used to think it was important to have a long life; but I let that go. Then I thought it was important to at least be able to grow up, get married and have kids; but I let that go. Then I decided that what was important in life was to be able to go to college and drive a car and have a girlfriend; I let that go, too. Finally I decided that health had to be the most important thing in life. But today I even had to give that up. Today I can see what is really important. The only thing that is important in life is love...how much love you give and how much love you receive."

The truth and simplicity of what he had said captured me. I was stunned by the poignancy of his next revelation: "That's why I'm so miserable now. I feel like I've never been able to give love or receive it." The desolation in his expression was so complete, so agonizing, it brought the whole world to a screeching halt. In that stillness, only he and I existed, and the ball was in my court.

I asked Arthur to answer these questions: At what age did he decide he was not lovable? Where was he? Who was he with? What was happening? What was being said?

He easily recalled a time when he was small, and it had seemed that his father had rejected him. He had drawn the conclusion that if his own father did not love him, he must not be lovable.

2

Looking back at the childhood scene with his 19 years of understanding, Arthur could now see that his father had not actually rejected him. His father had just lost his job, and had been in a turmoil over pressures and self-doubts. He feared that he could not provide for his large family. Lashing out at his boy was a misplaced expression of this fear, and not rejection at all. He had actually always loved Arthur.

Arthur now realized that he had resisted love for years for no reason. The whole mistake was built upon this simple misunderstanding.

I told him something I had learned from *A Course in Miracles*, " 'Love waits on welcome and not on time.' All of the love that you had is still with you, waiting to be let in. You could let it in now."

Arthur liked the idea. With a new life in his eyes, he announced his readiness to receive all the love that his friends always had for him through the years. He closed his eyes and opened his heart. He lay there quietly for some minutes, drinking in the sweetness and comfort of experiencing his friends' love. A hush of peace sweetened the air and made it fragrant with happiness.

Rousing, Arthur told me he was ready to receive the love of his family. Again he slipped into his inner experience, his eyelashes quiet on his cheeks. Time turned slow and thick. At first I wondered if he had fallen asleep. After a while he looked out at me and said, smiling, "Now I am ready to receive the love of God."

With that he again closed his eyes. The room softened with the innocence and beauty of great joy, to become a sanctuary with the holiness of a cathedral. A wave of bliss swept over Arthur's face, and in the minutes that followed, I said my silent farewell and left him in communion with his Creator.

The following morning the doctor called my office. "What did you tell Arthur yesterday?" he asked excitedly. At my hesitation, he quickly explained that at midnight he had received the ominous call from the nurse's station. Arthur was failing. The doctor had jumped in his car and raced to the hospital, but he was informed when he arrived that Arthur had already died.

He decided to enter the room where Arthur's body lay, wishing to say his last goodbye. When he reached the bed and looked down at the boy's face, he could not believe his eyes. He saw there the most beatific smile he had ever seen in his life. An expression of heartbreaking joy and exuberance communicated the transfiguration Arthur had experienced as he died. The doctor held the boy's spent body in his arms and cried the tears of loss, joy and hope.

This man had specialized in cancer treatment because he wanted to face his own fear of death. Arthur's joyful passage was the greatest gift he could have given his doctor. The gift I received from Arthur was the understanding that it is never too late to have a happy childhood.

Feel into your heart now, Sweetheart. Can you find it? And if you can, what do you find? It feels to me that you, too, like so many others, ache for love. You, too, have been mistaken about your worth, about how much you are valued, and how much you are loved.

Loved just for who you are, not for what you can do or become. You hunger to feel loved simply for being yourself. You need to feel it. And Love wants you just as dearly, just as much. Even more.

The Love of which I am speaking has only one goal, only one desire; a desire so much greater than we can even begin to imagine. It is the desire to draw us into the profound awareness of our Oneness with It.

This woman's hope for love was as great as yours....

NAGASAKI WOMAN

In the seminar room, the Nagasaki woman's face was plain and strong, yet a deep sensuality also lent it beauty. The Bomb had not taken her parents from her, but other tragedies had. She was orphaned at 13, and she had been working ever since.

Bright and industrious, she had won herself a nursing degree and independence. Now, so many years later, she ached from the loneliness of her solitary life. She was in love with a man she could not bring herself to approach. She wanted to share her life, to be loved, to be in a relationship. Through my interpreter, she asked what she could do.

I asked her if she denied herself this relationship because she could not imagine herself to be other than orphaned, abandoned, and alone. Had she never finished grieving the loss of her mother and father, never finished feeling the fear

5

and the anguish? Was it old pain that stood between her and happiness?

Yes.

Would she be willing to finish the grief of abandonment, so that she could end her compulsion to be alone? I asked.

Yes.

The woman stepped forward to the front of the room and seated herself beside me. Long suffering had deadened her eyes...her grief was far distant, buried, dissociated, and unremembered. She looked at me, empty but willing.

By focusing all of my attention on her I could make her be my all, my everything; she was not just the most important thing, not just more important than I, she became the entirety of existence. From here I could notice that I was the woman. We were the same, and I was forgotten, willing to be here, her, forever, no matter what.

Through the rapport, I swam into her, feeling for something of her to grasp, to hold onto, to know and experience. For two minutes we looked at each other as I searched for her heart. The other Japanese seminar participants watched, knowing from past experience just what would come.

At last, in my chest I could feel the roughness, the thickness of some repressed human experience, some emotion still too submerged in her unconscious to be defined. It was the start, a remnant, the first finger-hold. I could now begin to feel her heart with my own.

Then, oh!...aching sadness...loss.... The woman crumples forward, crying into her hands. Internally I reach into the denseness of her pain and pull it into the light.

A rush of fierce intensity sweeps through us, then the sweetness of inspiration, a wild exhilaration. We are *alive!* The Life demands all that is not right be righted, all that is hurt be made whole. She cries, then throws herself into my arms.

My eye catches movement in the group: agitated arms and legs, rocking bodies; the others are now deeply into their own healing. The seminar staff move to hold and support the participants who are tumbling through emotion the fastest. Almost everyone in the room is blinded by tears as the old, maybe even ancient, anguish of loneliness is released. Two of the men bellow the loudest. It is music, beauty, birth.

The emotion blows through my own heart like a jet stream. Exhilaration! Soon, the balance of emotion has made a noticeable shift. I can feel love. LOVE now! Love so great, so endless, so joyous and satisfying, so alive and sentient! I feel humility in its presence, but no self-consciousness. Gratitude, but not separation.

The shift has also taken place in the woman, and in the group mind. She still cries as I look into her eyes, but the tears come from the confrontation of love. Its beauty is almost too much to bear as it brings up all of the need, all of the lack. The group rocks with the impact, wails with the hunger.

Then, as I look on the woman, I am moved by a compassion that extends beyond her. Through her unknown and exotic face my eyes see the countless millions of Earth's children who live their lives with the same need, their hearts untouched, starving to be known. We are all one, connected, in truth just a single being!

My consciousness rises, and I sense the Angels or Friends–whoever they are–that are always just above our awareness, always reaching out to us with attention, vision and help. How amazing it is to know they care so much! Sweet communion, and then another shift.

A membrane inside me breaks. I am no longer myself, or no longer just myself. My consciousness lifts into the experience that, as a human being, I am one with Mother/ Father God. The woman, these children, are Ours. Precious beyond words, We love them. And through them I reach all of Our Own. I feel them receive Us...Fulfillment...Joy... Ecstasy...Oneness!

I hear laughter in the room, and I come back to myself. As I look, already many of the people are smiling, joyful, thankful, embracing and over-flowing. Turning again to the woman, I see that her eyes are filled with wonder.

"Thank you, thank you! I feel happy now!" She says in English.

In my heart I can feel the change in her. She is healed, whole, open, alive, and happy. Her life will never be the same.

Gratitude flows down to us from above. We are known, and the angels are dancing.

Let me take you back to the beginning, back to the Garden, before the fall, before the loss. See if this story stirs a half-forgotten remembrance in your own soul. A remembrance of peace and joy and ease, a memory of knowing your worth, a time of beauty and grace and love.

The Garden is real, and it ever awaits you. It is a state of mind that speaks to you of your innocence and safety. It is the reality of Heaven on earth, and it calls to you, Sweetheart, it calls your name....

THE FALL

The first time the lights went out I was only four or five years old. Until that time I enjoyed what anyone would call a happy childhood. Growing up in a farming community in Arizona, I knew a gentle existence. My memories of that time are all golden, as if I lived in the Garden of Eden before the fall from Grace.

I was carried through my days in a current of sweet and joyful energy, at the center of a beam of softly loving light. My body moved with an animal fluidity that was pure delight.

The best thing of all was the simple pleasure of enjoying who I was. It was great fun just to be me. Just to know how beautiful, wonderful, and lovable I was! I loved life and I loved myself. I was a little angel, living in a heavenly paradise, shining my light with great enthusiasm.

My parents' child-rearing approach was what my mother called "benevolent neglect." That meant I was free to spend my days as I wanted, loose in the gardens and fields of the countryside.

I would spend hours on end playing with the animals. My older brother kept me in full supply of snakes, lizards, horned toads, bees, scorpions, pigeons, doves, and jack rabbits.

In addition to dogs and pet chickens, we always had lots of outdoor cats. I knew and loved each of them thoroughly, and even learned to speak their language. I could, for example, perfectly duplicate the "brrrrr-ow" sound a mother cat makes to call her babies. This made it easy to call wild kittens to me for taming. I believed that the cats and I could really converse.

Most precious to me was a big surly orange tomcat named Peaches. Every day I would dress him up in doll clothes so that we could play house. After he was outfitted in a bonnet, a dress and panties (a round hole was discretely cut out in the back to accommodate his tail), I would seat him in my dolly's high chair for a feeding, or tuck a blanket under his little chin and push him in my baby buggy.

Looking back now I realize that the steely look he had in his eyes at those times was embarrassment. He was undoubtedly mortified that one of the other cats might see him in such a compromising position. Regardless, Peaches always maintained his dignity. He never resisted or complained, allowing me, in my innocence, to get away with treatment that he would never have tolerated from a grown-up.

My mother's garden, with its big shade trees, plots of flowers and berries, and soft sweet grass, was an oasis in that hot and dusty desert place. I spent much of my time just drinking in the forms, fragrances and colors of the flowers; squeezing the "faces" of the snapdragons to make them talk and sing...picking pansies and sweet peas to serve as enchanted dolls. Life was not just good, it was perfect.

One day, while standing in the middle of our front lawn, a profound wave of bliss came over me. I felt I would nearly burst from ecstasy. I immediately had a great desire to share this experience with my mother, and I took her to our living room couch to talk. I told her how good life was, and how much I enjoyed it.

Enthusiastically I gave her an analogy: It felt like Mondays. I told her Monday was my favorite day of the week because on Monday I had a whole week to play before I had to go to church on Sunday (sitting still in church for an hour on a hard bench was torture for me). It was my attempt at expressing just how open and exciting the week ahead appeared on a Monday; how full of promise, and how enticingly delicious it seemed.

Then it all went wrong. The look on my mother's face became closed and hard. "No," she responded, "Life isn't that easy. You don't really get to be happy like that until you die and go to Heaven."

Did she really say that? I know that if you asked her today she would deny it. She was a good person. I think she was hoping to protect me from the disillusionment my brother went through when he first encountered the "real" world of a spiritually impoverished parochial school. Better that she break the bad news about life to me herself.

Tragically, instead of bringing my mother into my experience of bliss, I made some other kind of decision. It was a decision that threw me out of Heaven. It was my fall from Grace.

I remember the actual visual and physical sensation of falling down a dark tunnel of black clouds. As I tumbled, spiraling further and further from the light, anguishing in despair and loss, I heard a voice in my head say, quite analytically, "That was the stupidest thing I have ever done."

I remember nothing after that. It was as if I lost consciousness. I do not remember ever waking up.

My life thereafter was quite a different story. I began to believe that I was about the ugliest child that ever walked the planet. I developed phobias, compulsions, and facial tics. I walked in my sleep, wet my bed, and complained of stomach pains. Worst of all was the sense that there was something wrong with me. Something so basically part of my nature that people could not even perceive it.

It felt like an emptiness, a crippling shyness. When I was with other children I could never truly relax or be spontaneous; I did not even feel as if I was inside my body. Instead, it felt as if I stood a couple of feet behind myself, watching myself interact with them. I never experienced true contact, never lost self-consciousness and never again was I swept away with pure delight and happiness.

There have been a number of times throughout my life when the "lights went out." Adolescence was a particularly difficult time. In the course of one year I experienced devastating heartbreak, date rape, abortion, condemnation and ostracism. With each trauma, I would see my ability to perceive light literally dim, as if some of the lights in the room just burned out. Life became dark.

I believed I had broken every commandment in the Bible and made just about every stupid mistake a kid from a small town could make. I was doomed. I believed I would never find my way back to the Garden.

Your most basic, inalienable right as a human being, Sweetheart, is to know yourself. Devote yourself to that goal. Enlightenment, or Self-Realization, is simply that: realizing who you are, knowing your Self, keeping no secrets from yourself. But you have forgotten your innocence, your beauty.

Do not allow the powerful current of life to defeat you and cause you to give up on yourself. Do not lose your boldness, your willingness to risk, to dare, to LIVE....

THE JOURNEY TO HAPPINESS

I left home at the age of 18 to attend the University of Arizona. By the time I arrived there, I was far from being the natural, joyful child of my earliest years. I arrived in Tucson a heartbroken, mortified, and damaged young woman.

In an effort to "be accepted" and to "just get by," I had censored so many of my qualities, and denied so much of my experience and feelings, it seemed that more of me was hidden below the surface than found freedom above it.

About all that was left of me was a sweet, polite and helpful good student. I felt utterly and disgustingly bored with myself. Although I had a boyfriend and friends, I felt lonely. I had so many blessings, but no capacity to feel happy. Too much of me had been sacrificed in attempts to please others. I held up unnatural, plastic pretences as a mask to the world, and did not even realize I was not being real. I had become so hidden I knew very little about myself.

After attending a few years of college, I finally realized that I was majoring in psychology because I needed help. The fact that I silently wept through many of my psych classes should have been a dead giveaway. I entered therapy at the university counseling center my senior year, and began the messy process of clearing out my old pain, so that I could re-discover who I really was.

I had so much emotion that wanted to burst out of its prison, all I had to do was walk into my psychologist's waiting room for the tears to start to flow. I saw him every Friday afternoon for three months, each time releasing enormous amounts of emotion: anger, resentment, sadness, hurt, embarrassment, disappointment and loneliness. I was so exhausted after each session that I went straight home to bed, and stayed there all weekend until I had to pull myself together to attend classes on Mondays.

We did some Gestalt Therapy, some dream work, a little of this and that, but mostly he gently pushed me into admitting that I had feelings about things that I was not facing. He did not care much for the person I had made of myself, so a defensive part of me fought him, and made him the enemy. I transferred my authority conflict onto him...he was my parents, he was Barry Goldwater, he was heartless. But was he ever helpful!

I remember my last counseling session the best. I look back with respect and awe when I reflect on the amount of trust and caring my therapist demonstrated in the risk he took that day.

When I entered the counseling office for my session, I sat and composed myself for the work I expected to do. Then I looked at the psychologist, waiting for him to speak. He looked right back at me, a determined, set look on his face. He reached towards me, and without warning or provoca-tion, he shoved me back against my chair!

I responded with an exclamation of surprise, which he met with another shove. Soon he was shoving me all around the room! I tried talking with him, reasoning with him, questioning him, but, answering me only with a little smile, he would not stop. He wanted a physical fight, and finally, pushed past my breaking point, he got it.

I jumped him, and we wrestled for our lives the whole hour. Deceivingly frail in appearance, I had long denied my natural strength and pugnacity. The therapist's bullying had managed to rouse an angry aggressiveness in me which liberated a tidal wave of emotion.

In the face of my power, self-deception regarding my weakness, impotence and helplessness had to burn away. The man outweighed me by 50 or 60 pounds, but I opened up my natural strength and mopped up the office with him.

Much of that battle is a blur now, but I remember clearly, at the end, pinning his shoulders to the floor with my knees, my hands trapping his wrists uselessly above his head. He had fought with all his strength, given it everything he had, and lost to me.

We surrendered for a few moments to our need to catch our breath, glaring at each other eyeball to eyeball. Then a strange thing happened. My therapist began to laugh. Peals of laughter, belly laughs of pure delight, as he rolled around on the floor! And all I could do was watch, my mouth hanging open. As he stood up and dusted himself off, he announced that we had finished therapy together, and he thrust me out the door. He must have known he tossed me into a totally new world.

All I could deal with was the distinct sensation of having just been born. The lawn and walkways outside the Psych Department were visually brighter, more vivid, and in better focus. I had tumbled into the realm of experiencing feelings without apology, of tasting the vital force of my true nature without attempting to kill it or hide it.

I felt the dawning of realization: how little I knew about who I really was; how little I was aware of what I authentically felt; how much I wanted to be real. And I set my course.

Some challenges are so profound, so unimaginably difficult to overcome, that many who have faced them have lost their faith in Life. Yet challenges hold great power within them. All of your challenges hold power, Sweetheart. They are gifts of empowerment in a raw unfinished form, there to be won or lost.

BEAUTY OF THE HUMAN SPIRIT

My first vocational goal in college was to become a psychologist. To my disappointment, the psychology program at my university was "behaviorally" slanted, which translated into a strong emphasis on the study of rats in mazes.

Then one day I discovered that the university offered free vocational aptitude testing. I took the battery of tests to discover what I was really cut out to do. The results from these tests stated very clearly that I should become a vocational rehabilitation counselor. I was not completely sure what that meant, but I knew that it meant I would not be studying rats for another six years. So I changed my major, and began taking courses that would lead to Bachelor's and Master's degrees in rehabilitation counseling.

The first thing I discovered when I started my "rehab" courses was that there were a number of physically disabled students in my program. Oddly, you might think, this was distressing to me. I had noticed these students in their wheel chairs and braces, "littering" the campus with their pain and imperfections; stories too horrible to hear, losses too dramatic to imagine as personal. I had not known many disabled people before, and I did not feel comfortable around them.

I felt embarrassed and awkward, afraid that they would resent that I was able-bodied. I hated to imagine myself in their shoes. I felt the whole gamut of unpleasant emotions as I had to sit next to them.

Then, as they became real people I knew, I could not help but notice just how attractive the disabled students were. Not necessarily attractive in the physical sense, since many times their physical bodies were strange and even frightening. One young man's face was so disfigured that he was startling to look at. Many of them were in wheelchairs. Some on crutches. Some deaf, some blind. Yet all of them had a brilliance inside. A happiness. A light inside that showed them to be somehow and for some reason, more sterling than the rest of us. More fine, more polished, more "cool." Just, in many ways, more beautiful.

Soon I found myself proud to be counted as their friend. I very much enjoyed my time with them. In fact, one of these students (a fellow who had been restricted to a wheelchair since his early youth), became my best friend throughout my remaining university years. I came to realize that the beauty that shone out of these individuals, that poured out of their hearts and minds, was the beauty that comes from success-fully meeting a challenge. They had profited from triumph.

One fellow who had been born with cerebral palsy had to have the muscles to his knees severed so that his legs did not curl up. His legs thereafter were ponderous weights that he strapped into braces each day with hands that he could barely control. Then he would drag himself from class to class across the campus on his crutches, rain or shine, while also carrying his books in a backpack. For him to turn a page of a textbook took tremendous concentration and effort. To take a bath, to shave, or to comb his hair took hours of time and effort and courage. He never once complained, or called attention to his challenges. He was a wonderful man, funny as a whip, and totally heroic.

I do not believe that he or the others necessarily started out being all that phenomenal. I believe that, like the rest of us, they were born with the potential for greatness. During their lives, they were given a challenge that offered the opportunity to discover their greatness, and their beauty. Many people with similar tests have been lost to bitterness and defeat; but these souls had evolved into a deeper, wiser and tempered form of human.

I could not have valued their friendship more. It began to create an appetite inside me to experience human beings at their very best, at their most beautiful. In response to challenge, these people demonstrate just how gorgeous a human heart can be; how much courage we can muster; how much faith, hope, compassion and love we can express; how much maturity it is possible to attain.

*Give up your right to withhold yourself, Sweet-
heart. People's very lives may be at risk...their
hearts depending on you to find them, to open the
way for them, to bring them to life.*

*For you, the price of your withholding is ter-
rible. For the world, it is intolerable.*

*Listen inside to what is true for you to do, then
take a risk! Give the gifts that only you can give....*

ARROGANCE

Between my junior and senior years in undergraduate
school, I attended a total immersion language program in
Guadalajara, Mexico. My intention was to learn the Spanish
language quickly and authentically. I wanted to capture the
accent and colloquialisms of genuine Mexican Spanish.

I lived with a Mexican family that spoke no English, ran
with a group of Mexican teenagers, and took courses on the
Spanish language and the Mexican culture. Thinking I could
squeeze in one additional course to get the most out of my
experience, I also signed up for an education class.

My first and only day of that course is highly memorable.
The instructor planned to base his course on the value of
group work (individuals interacting in small groups). He
would then apply this concept to the field of language
education.

He began the class with an exercise. He handed out a
sheet of paper which instructed us to imagine that on a
rocket-ship flight we had crash-landed and were stranded on
the moon. He listed 30 objects that were unrelated and
widely different in their purpose and use, things such as an
inner tube, a magnet, a bottle of beer, a blanket.

We were to list these objects by rank in regard to their
priority of value. The object of most value to a person

stranded on the moon would be at the head of the list, and the object of least value at the end. We were to pretend that our lives depended on our decisions. He gave us 20 minutes to work on the exercise individually. At the end of that time, he assigned us each to a small group of six.

We were then to share with the group our individual rankings of the objects and discuss why we rated them in that order. Then we were to come up with a group consensus of which items we would most need in order to survive as a group if stranded on the moon.

After a given period of time he gave us the correct answers as determined by a group of scientists. We were instructed to score our individual attempts, and then to score our group results.

At the end, each of the groups were asked their score. Our group scored a fairly high rating. The instructor announced that the object of the whole exercise was this: no individual in the entire class was to have scored as high as their own group scored. His point was that in every case, six heads would be better than one.

When I looked at my individual score, and our group score, the case was reversed. My individual score was almost perfect. My group's score was far below my own. In fact, my individual score was way above the highest group score. When I told this to the instructor, he blew a fuse. He began to yell at me.

How dare I, when in possession of superior knowledge and ability, sit on those resources just to be polite? When other people's lives depended on it! How dare I be so arrogant! How dare I be so self-centered and foolish! What an idiot I was! And with a look that suggested he wanted to spit, he kicked me out of his class, telling me not to return. He did not want a person like me as his student.

The experience was embarrassing, even humiliating. Yet I felt grateful. It was a kick that I needed and profited from.

I learned more in that one day than I could have hoped to have learned in a whole semester of classes.

I stopped apologizing for my presence in groups. I gave myself permission to give as much as I could, and to help in whatever way possible. The gifts that are mine to give, if not given by me, will never be given.

There is no order of difficulty in miracles. One is not "harder" or "bigger" than another. They are all the same. All expressions of love are maximal.

A Course in Miracles, Text, p. 1

CHEATING

I started my first professional job, Supervisor of Counseling for an agency serving deaf and hearing-impaired people, while I was still in graduate school. It was a wonderful job in a wonderful program, and I was intrigued with the work.

I had started learning sign language in undergraduate school, thinking that the skill would make me more employable. When doing volunteer work with deaf people I was able to practice their language and learn their culture. I became captivated by their dilemma: although deaf people fit into the normal bell-shaped curve of intelligence, most function far below their intellectual capacity.

It is extremely difficult to learn to read and write the English language if you cannot hear it. Learning to speak it without hearing it is even more difficult. The resulting communication barrier creates functional illiteracy and social isolation for most deaf persons.

Since the majority of deaf people were born to parents who could hear but never learned sign language ("experts" advised against it), the inability to learn to communicate and relate with those closest to them set them up for additional social challenges. The profile of deaf people as a group is one of great underdeveloped potential.

In school I was trained in assisting deaf people to become more independent in the mainstream culture through providing education, vocational training and job placement. There was nothing said about actually counseling deaf people. The state of the art of counseling for them appeared to be solving their immediate problems, and coordinating services with other agencies.

Therapists without fluency in sign language and an understanding of deaf culture could do little to help, and could actually do damage through misdiagnosis and incorrect treatment (what are normal behaviors, beliefs, facial expressions, etc. in the deaf culture would not be seen as normal in the "hearing" culture). There were no guidelines for assisting deaf people to free themselves from the pain of their inner lives.

The clients in my caseload were deaf people who had additional disabling physical or mental conditions. Some of their situations were incredibly challenging. For example, one client was a deaf, blind, psychotic, gay, obese, diabetic, suicidal black man who was repeatedly mugged after I taught him how to use a white cane (the cane alerted thugs to the fact that he was blind and defenseless). These were people with desperate stories and devastating disabilities.

Conventional rehabilitation services were not helping. The whole situation made me mad enough to be willing to reach beyond anything I had ever been taught, to reach beyond myself. I developed the willingness to find the part of me that knew miracles could happen. Soon we began to allow something very interesting to happen in our sessions, behind the closed door of my office.

I developed therapeutic methods for visual language that helped the clients examine their thought processes. These techniques I could readily teach to others. What I kept from my co-workers and students was something I could not at that time explain: my clients' emotional problems were healing rapidly. They were healed by a miraculous state of mind; I *willed* them to change.

My heart was developing the ability to drop the barrier of bodies and to reach into my clients' hearts to join with them. And while we were joined, I willed them to be healthy, strong and happy.

Watching the dramatic results, I became frightened that I was cheating somehow, afraid it might be wrong to have so much influence over others. Yet my clients' happiness, success, and emotional freedom spoke loudly to me. In my heart I accepted responsibility for what I was doing, and decided to continue.

Things went along fine until one day another counselor referred her client to me. He was a tall, beautiful, strapping young Hispanic man. With his wire-rimmed glasses and long hair he looked like the other students on the university campus.

His emotional development had been arrested due to abuse he had received from the deaf school's nurse (whenever he was "naughty" in class, she would lock him in her closet–sometimes for hours). This had caused him to be quiet and repressed and very shy with females. He had never had a girlfriend. Fortunately, his intelligence and his written English language skills made it possible for him to function rather well in a "hearing" world, and to do well in his course work.

The counselor had referred this young man to me because she did not have the courage to tell him something that his doctor also did not have the courage to tell him. He was slowly being blinded by a disease called retinitis pigmentosa. Within a year or two he would be both deaf and blind. He would not even be able to work in the field he had been studying in school. Years of effort had been wasted, and he would not be able to do what he had wanted to do with his life.

Imagine what it would be like to go through life both deaf and blind! To have to be *that* dependent on others. Deaf people are typically terrified of becoming blind. It is their worst nightmare. I decided that the only way to be told such dire news was by someone at very close range.

I felt that if I could get close enough to him when I gave him his diagnosis, if I could establish enough rapport and intimacy, somehow I could help. I cannot remember quite what I said to him during that counseling session, but a miracle happened. When he walked out of my office, he felt so inspired about meeting the new challenge of blindness that he had a big grin on his face.

I was dumbfounded that a human being could feel so happy just minutes after receiving such news. I was afraid the happiness would not last, that he might fall out of it, and land in a deep depression when he was all alone.

I need not have worried. At a follow-up session two weeks later he was still cheerfully (even boisterously) optimistic. What was even more amazing to me was that he had brought a lovely buxom deaf co-ed along for me to meet. This boy who had never even kissed a girl before had fallen in love. The two were living together and planning a life together. He had chosen a new major in school, and was excited about his new direction in life. He was totally "turned on" (to use a phrase of the time) about his future.

This was too much. The miracle of it frightened me to the core. Was it all right to have that much influence on another person's life? The power of it was too scary.

Within two weeks I had resigned my counseling job and had administrative work lined up in Hawaii, thousands of miles away. It was a long time before I felt the courage and worthiness to accept and develop the power of the heart.

Fear is a powerful means of holding yourself in denial, preventing you from using your abilities to help heal humanity. Accept the challenge of receiving miracles, so that others may find their wholeness, and you may find your own.

You may think that in comparison with some others you have little to complain about, Sweetheart, but much of your heart has been lost to you. You hunger for your natural state of love and joy.

A great wealth lies buried in your heart and mind, buried in memories of grief or pain. It is your treasure, waiting only to be refined and claimed!

The parts of your life that you pulled away from long ago hold you hostage now, demanding one thing only: acknowledgment.

Once you acknowledge what you feel, the old emotions will release you. And in the process you will gain the treasure that comes from life fully lived—wisdom and maturity.

Life's confrontation is a process that will free you from the pain that stopped you in the past...since the pain of the present is only the pain of the past revisited. Feel everything that life shakes loose in you so that you may become free to be yourself....

BUSTED

When I moved to Honolulu at the age of 25, I discovered myself to be a big fish in a small pond. It was a wonderful opportunity to gain experience I would not normally have had the chance to acquire at my age. I wrote grants, started new agencies and training programs, worked with the mayor, the governor and the legislature, and soon was given a high-level job with the state government. In short, I had just about everything a status-seeking, career-minded young woman could want.

Since I had become an administrator, I no longer counseled deaf people. Instead, I served as a liaison between the deaf community and the "system." I felt good about everything I was accomplishing, and enjoyed my relationships with the deaf people and my position in the community.

From time to time I brought in renowned experts on deafness from around the U.S. to assist us in setting and accomplishing our goals. One such expert, a bright and militant deaf man from Washington, D.C. assessed our situation. I expected he would be pleased and impressed with everything that was occurring. At the end of his visit he said to me, "The deaf people of Hawaii look to you as their Savior. Just be sure you never see yourself that way."

I was hurt that he could say such a thing to me, when it was obvious that I was such a "good guy." It was at least 24 hours before I had the courage to really examine what he had said.

What I saw when I took an honest look inside myself turned my stomach. I saw my need for approval, need to be needed, need to rescue and to be a hero, and need to be important. I felt I had exploited the deaf people to serve my own illusion of myself as a Helper. I was doing "good," but the good I was doing, at least in part, was to make me more glamorous.

Once again I faced the cold, hard truth: I did not know myself. I did not understand why I did the things I did. In how many ways was I doing the right things for the wrong reasons?

The old desire began to grow in me, slowly at first, but building and generating through the years. It was the desire to know myself.

Truthfully, I am often distressed and embarrassed to discover my repressed and hidden character flaws and weakness. Perhaps knowing that others can see these aspects of me, whether I see them or not, motivates me to keep "busting" myself. After all, if something about my character or personality is evident to everyone else, I want to know about it, too. It is less embarrassing than not knowing, and the truth is, people do not see us as we want to be seen.

Each of us has developed into a character–a hero or heroine, a clown, a tragic figure, a villain, a winner, a loser, or some other illusion. We did it because we thought it was easier or safer or smarter to be the illusion than to be our real self. The roles are shallow, empty, and hollow compared to the richness of our real selves.

And the funny thing about these made-up characters is that we're the only ones that really fall for them. We all see through each other's illusions, but not our own. Self-discovery can be a fairly shocking process.

A fascinating thing happens, however, every time I do face up to an unpleasant aspect of myself. As soon as I recognize it and own it enough to say, "Yes, I'm like that," and feel the emotion related to it, the offensive quality disappears. Actually, it does not really disappear. It becomes integrated into the rest of my self-knowledge and serves as an asset rather than a disability.

The "bitch" in me, when acknowledged and integrated, becomes an ability to be assertive. The "judger" becomes discerning, the "selfish one" becomes self-caring, etc.

Even though many self-revelations have been shocking and difficult to face at the time, the experiences, in the long run, clearly have improved my self-concept. False self-images are painful and detrimental and provide no nourishment. True self-knowledge builds self-esteem.

So far I have only talked about the shock of facing "negative" aspects of self. The amazing thing is that we are equally, if not more, resistant to discovering "positive" qualities about ourselves. Both involve being willing to be wrong about ourselves. As *A Course in Miracles* says, we would prefer to be right than happy. I think the whole growth process amounts to being willing to be wrong about who we think we are.

Your loneliness is your heart's desire to grow in its capacity to know true Oneness and intimacy.
Accept your life path, with all of its struggles, as the vehicle through which you are to learn the nature of truth.

SETTLING

Living in Honolulu was not as idyllic as you might think. I found it a lonely place to live. The Island culture did not welcome outsiders, and I found that most of the friends I made were recent arrivals like myself.

It was such a difficult place for mainland "haoles" like me to live that most of us did not stay long. It seemed that as soon as I made a friend they were gone. I had never lived at the receiving end of racial discrimination before, and I hurt from the isolation.

After a couple of months, I found a nice young man, another new arrival, to date. He worked in the field of rehabilitation also, and we enjoyed having each other as a friend in all of the professional meetings we needed to attend.

We never felt a real romance–the kind of state where you want to know everything about the other person. We found little to talk about. I do not know if we would ever have begun dating if we had lived somewhere on the mainland, but here we needed each other. No one else came along for us to date, and so we lived more and more as partners.

Then one night we found ourselves planning our lives around each other. With surprise we wondered, did this mean that we should be getting married? It certainly would make our families happy, wouldn't it? And wouldn't life be more interesting, more grown up, more worth living?

Secretly, I think we had both given up on having romance, on falling in love. We had both had our hearts broken early in our teens. We did not really expect to ever be able to feel that "in love" feeling again. Shouldn't we settle for marriage to a nice person? A good and kind person? Someone with whom to share expenses and income and build a future?

And so, without a proposal, without joy, we decided to marry. A wedding would be fun, wouldn't it?

In our pre-marriage counseling session the minister advised against the wedding. He felt that we did not really want to get married–or at least we did not want it enough. We did not know what he was talking about.

Two weeks before the big day, we became aware of a feeling pressing on our minds. Dread. We should not be getting married! What were we thinking? Yet the invitations had been mailed! The arrangements had been made! What would our families feel if we backed out? How could we embarrass everyone? How could we embarrass ourselves? Better to go ahead with the plans. Oh, my God. Trapped!

The wedding itself was lovely. I did not realize at the time why I had chosen Bach's Little Fugue in G Minor (a funeral dirge) to accompany my father and myself as we marched down the aisle. My new husband came down with a terrible sore throat and ear infection on our wedding night. At the time I felt it was a subconscious reaction to hearing words he did not want to hear and saying words he did not want to say.

A doctor had to visit us at our hotel room before we could leave on our honeymoon. It was a lonely trip we took to Oaxaca, Mexico. It seemed like the end of the earth.

Time moved on, and we adjusted to our life together. We were good roommates; we never fought. We merely encountered each other in our apartment, never really connecting at an emotional level.

Looking for some excitement, I planned another trip. We would travel to New Zealand, stopping for a few days to explore Fiji on the way. It would be exotic and fun!

When we got off the plane in Fiji we were met by a solid wall of water falling from the sky; the monsoon season had arrived early. It would be five straight days of rain, stuck in a hotel where there was nothing to do. And, since we were there together, there was no one to talk to.

The hotel guests congregated in the grass thatched hotel bar to stare out at the downpour. I was not a drinker, but my husband began to drink quite a bit out of boredom. On the third day a strange thing occurred.

My husband, who had become quite drunk, looked directly at me. A change came over him. His speech no longer slurred, he spoke with clarity and intensity. His voice even sounded different, as if someone else or a different part of himself was speaking.

"We were never supposed to be married," he said. "It was a mistake. There is another man you are supposed to be with. A good man. You and he have work to do together." Then he was silent, and returned to watching the rain.

The next day, when my husband was sober, I questioned him about that conversation. He had no memory of what he had said.

The life you are living in the world is truly only a metaphor for the life you are living inside your beliefs and your thoughts. There is a way to view your world from a different perspective, one that opens your mind to new meaning, and changes everything–your whole life–in a way that makes any event meaningful. Do you want to live an adventure, Sweetheart?

A NEW PARADIGM

The most profound paradigm shift I have ever experienced came in answer to my puzzling about the meaning of life. I remember when the actual shift to the new model took place. I had been reading everything I could get my hands on about metaphysics, depth psychology, holistic health, psychic phenomena, world religions and spiritual masters.

I had all the pieces to a completely new picture, one radically different in every way from my old view, if my mind had the courage to conceive of it. Yet this answer stayed tantalizingly out of reach, teasing me with its nearness, while frustrating me with its intangibility.

I was walking down a busy Honolulu street, mentally digesting two books I had just read (*Illusions,* by Richard Bach, and *The Handbook of Higher Consciousness,* by Ken Keyes). As I walked and pondered, an astonishing change took place inside of my head. Some threshold of understanding or "critical mass" was reached, and my mind stopped, unable to continue.

It stood perched on a fence; on one side was my familiar world with its grip of inertia and the ingrained beliefs of a lifetime...while on the other side was a whole new world, a radically different way of seeing things, a new way of living, an exciting frontier! The two paradigms were as different as night and day. They excluded each other so totally that I would have to choose one or the other. Then, somewhere inside me a decision was reached, a new understanding dawned, and for a few moments I experienced the magnificence of human intelligence.

Through my mind's need for integrity and consistency, the new thought communicated with all my existing beliefs, and countless debates ensued. Faster than any computer could have operated, a tally was reached: overwhelming support for the new way of seeing things! I had the sensation of countless pieces of shattered mind falling apart and rearranging themselves in a new order, much like the shuffling that takes place in front of your eye when you twist a kaleidoscope.

I looked out with new eyes on a strange yet wonderful kingdom, as different from my old world as Oz is from Kansas. Life/Mind showed Its startling face to me where I had seen only ordinariness before.

Where once I had automatically seen a world of objects "out there," and "other" people, now I looked out and saw myself. Nothing but myself, as I was expressed through people, places, things, and events.

All of the hidden aspects of myself–the secret guilt, the merciless judgements, the pain, the needs–were all seen finding freedom of expression outside of me in my relationships and experiences. I no longer saw other people's conflicts, dilemmas or attacks on me as "their problem," or "their stuff."

If I could see it in my world, it was a hint about a hidden issue inside me. I comprehended that every event in my life was meaningful (the meaning being what my own mind ascribed to it). Nothing happened by chance. My world was nothing more than a reflection of my consciousness–looking at the world was like looking into a mirror.

Just as I knew my mind populated its nighttime dreams with comprehendible symbols of my self-concept, I saw that my mind found the same artistic expression while awake. Everything, *everything*, was me. I could know myself by reading the events that unfolded around me. For the first time since I was a child, I understood the trick and illusion of life.

I could see the whole world as being completely my perception, entirely malleable, existing only for me. It was my invention. If I changed who I was, changed my beliefs, changed my inner life, the world outside of me would change simultaneously; there was a direct correlation.

I felt awe at the magnificence of the world as a learning device. Ultimately responsible for all that took place in my world, I was also ultimately powerful to change and create, and to heal my world by healing myself.

Miracles are associated with fear only because of the belief that darkness can hide. You believe that what your physical eyes cannot see does not exist. This leads to a denial of spiritual sight.

A Course in Miracles, Text, p. 2

EXPERTS

From what I have seen, when people make a shift into a different paradigm they experience a surge of energy and enthusiasm much like the "high" of falling in love. It is an exciting time.

My paradigm shift was accompanied by an opening to a whole new level of physical and spiritual experiences. I had visions, out-of-body experiences, past-life memories (however one explains those), and spontaneous kundalini awakenings (a real surprise to the uninitiated). I had to deal with my pounding fear of the unknown, but I was confronted only with beauty, love and, for lack of a better description, cosmic intelligence.

When these experiences first began, I did not quite know what to make of them. I wanted to be sure that they were a sign of health and not of delusion or illness (by the way, not only did I not use drugs or alcohol, I would not even drink anything with caffeine). I decided to get input from some experts.

I felt that talking about visions and psychic experiences would likely open too big of a can of worms by triggering people's prejudices and fears. So I decided to investigate a less threatening symptom, that of seeing colored lights move like liquid across my field of vision whenever I relaxed and closed my eyes.

The primary color was blue, the color of nighttime marker lights on airport runways (later, the predominate color would be a bright violet, and I would also see constantly moving spangles of white light, dancing through tiny crystalline formations).

Occasionally, when deeply in rapport with someone, I would see the colored light travel in puffs from me to the person I was relating to, even when my eyes were open. If meditating, I could take a ride outward on one of those puffs into an out-of-body experience.

I took this symptom to my physician, an internist, first. His first question was to ask me if I meditated. He said he used to meditate in his karate class, and occasionally he would see a bit of light like that. He smiled, patted my back and said, "It's a good thing."

I visited a chiropractor who told me that I was experiencing increased energy flow up my spine. The colored light was a good thing.

My ophthalmologist, a gentleman of retirement age, smiled wisely at me, patted me on the back and said, "It's a signpost of higher consciousness. It's a very, very good thing."

To get a mental health read-out, I went to a psychologist available through my health plan. He had no prior exposure to the phenomena I was encountering. In the first session I told him everything I could about my various "other dimensional" experiences. He had me visit him six times before he was willing to give me his professional read-out.

In the sixth session, he told me that he thought I was perfectly healthy. Had another person given him this information, he might not have believed them. Since it came from me, he believed that what was happening was valid, and he stated that he thought it was important for his colleagues to learn about it.

He asked for books about out-of-body experiences to share with the other therapists in his office. I wonder what they made of it all.

In your soul abides true wisdom, and authentic spiritual power and presence. Seek contact with it, Sweetheart, as it is seeking you.

Miracles reawaken the awareness that the spirit, not the body, is the altar of truth. This is the recognition that leads to the healing power of the miracle.

A Course in Miracles, Text, p. 2

MERRILY, MERRILY

Perhaps the most mind-boggling event I had ever experienced occurred the evening that I "woke up" from life. I actually found myself waking up from this life as if it were nothing but a dream...much like the kind of dream I normally have at night when I am asleep.

While I am having a nighttime dream, everything seems real to me. I buy it. I believe it. I believe that the dream is reality and that those experiences are really happening to me. Even though the things that happen in my nighttime dreams are not as logical as the things that happen when I am "awake," still, while I'm dreaming, I believe that the dream is real.

As I wake up, when I'm right on the cusp, right between being asleep and being awake, there is just a little bit of confusion. There is the question, "Well, what is real?" Then I realize, "Oh, now I'm awake, this is real, and that was just a dream."

The nighttime dream, the sleeping dream, just dissolves. It withdraws back into the depths of my mind, and for all intents and purposes is lost to me. I may remember a few things about it, if it was an especially interesting dream for some reason or another. Because I do not value my dreams all that much, they evaporate like wisps of mist, and there is nothing left of them anymore. I become completely engaged in my "real" life, and I believe that this is what's real and important, and this is what I need to pay attention to.

Then one evening, I had the experience of going to bed and to sleep, but as I dreamed, a vibration swept over me. I awakened–not in my normal reality, not in my normal life, but in another reality entirely. This reality was much lovelier, happier, and brighter. It was as if I had awakened sitting on the lawns of a Garden of Eden or a Heavenly world. It was as different from this life that I normally think of as reality, as my nighttime dreams are different from my daytime experiences.

During this "waking up" from my normal reality, I went through that same type of experience of being on the cusp. Looking back, I was able to remember myself as Lency. I could remember my family, friends, and the circumstances of my life. As I began to awaken more, and the fog began to leave my mind, I remembered that in fact *that* was not who I was at all. That was just a dream. And being just a dream it had very little importance to me.

So I let it go and allowed it to recede back into my mind as a dream does. Because after all, it was just a dream, it was not real. This reality where I had awakened was so much more sane, so much more brilliantly beautiful, *so much more vividly real.* "How could I ever have believed that dream was really happening?" I wondered, amazed.

Unfortunately I was not able to stay in that Garden for long. After a little while, to my great disappointment, I found myself pulled back, back into my ordinary reality. That brief experience taught me something that is really beyond value. When the major world religions talk about life being just a dream, they are not speaking of a metaphor or using a euphemistic teaching device. It is very seriously the truth. This life is nothing but a dream.

Your spirit strives to draw you into an awakened state. You are journeying toward enlightenment and the realization of your true nature.

All of life on this earth is a school of experience that points in only one direction...Homeward, Heavenward.

*Transformation is the process of healing your
separation from Love.*

*No matter how many blessings you have in your
life, Sweetheart, if you are missing a connection to
the infinite Source of Love, you will feel empty,
alone, and finite.*

THE SUPPORT CENTER

Two goals were forming in my mind. The first related to
my hunger for information and experiences that would
expand my new insights. Almost all of my free time was spent
reading and attending lectures and workshops. I decided to
create a job in which I could be paid for learning what I
wanted to learn, and I set my intention.

The second goal was related to a private shame, my best-
kept secret. My secret was that, to my great dismay, I was
unable to love. My heart felt as immobile and dead as stone.

I doubted if many people suspected my handicap since my
false character was very solicitous and caring. It was
distressingly evident in my inner life that I had lost my human
ability to feel love. I wanted to heal my heart, to regain the
experience of life there, to be able to *feel.* Again I set my
intention.

In my next daily meditation I saw the face of the local
Unity Church minister and felt drawn to write him of my
situation and my desire to create new employment working
with children and metaphysics. By return mail I received a
letter from him which remarked on the great coincidence of
receiving my message.

He was working with some physicians and community
leaders to create a support program for children with life-
threatening illnesses and their families, based on the metaphysical teachings found in *A Course in Miracles.* They had

just decided that the program should be designed and run by a paid director. He asked me to apply for the job when I saw the ad in the paper.

I told my supervisor at work that I had set my sights on working with the support program, and told him why. I wanted him to have the earliest possible warning that I would be leaving. I began closing down my work, and packed my books and files during breaks. Eighty people applied for the director's job when it was advertised. I never once doubted that it was "my" job, created for me.

When I was hired as the Executive Director for the new Young People's Support Center, most of my friends and colleagues were shocked and concerned about me working directly with dying children. Many gave me advice about how to shield myself from the experience so I would not have to feel pain and heartbreak. I smiled and nodded at their advice, not revealing that I wanted to have my heart broken open.

I wanted to be able to feel again, and I believed that being undefended in the presence of kids whose greatest desire was to live would confront the parts of me that were dead or did not care about living. I knew that the children would find their way into my heart and open it.

I wanted to feel all of it. I wanted to feel all of me. It was really scary.

Do you ever fear that you will never find a life truly worth living? Trust the process of life, even when it becomes unpleasant or difficult. You are propelled through circumstances in direct alignment with your purpose, if you maximize each opening to growth.

CHUCK

The Support Center was to be fashioned from concepts from *A Course in Miracles* (a self-study spiritual and psychological system). As I was not yet a student of the *Course*–which was, I could already tell, an immense piece of intelligence to begin to digest–I went for the total immersion approach.

In addition to studying the material on my own, I began to meet with a newly forming *A Course in Miracles* study group. We were an outrageous gathering. There was myself (at age 28, the ingénue of the group), a gay hairdresser, a Catholic nun, a "rascally" middle-aged high school English teacher who dated his students, and a Japanese ophthalmologist who attended our meetings wearing a three-piece suit (one of the few suits on the island). We thought it tremendously funny that we should all have something deeply in common, and would sometimes go out after the meetings just to be seen together. We had a deep connection and great respect and affection for one another.

We felt that we were perfect study partners. Being so different, each of us applying the course lessons to our lives brought up diverse insights and anecdotes to share with the others each week.

Occasionally other people would drift through our group. One Chinese woman named Lynette joined us, but immediately fell into a power struggle with the men in the group. After a couple of weeks she dropped out but, because she liked me, she took my phone number. She and I had both been experiencing "deadness" in our marriages, and she thought that we should get together sometime to talk.

Lynette did not call–not for four months. Then one night at 11 o'clock (that's *late* in Hawaii) the phone rang. Awakening from a deep sleep, it took me awhile to figure out who the heck "Lynette" was. She was mortified to have been so rude as to wake me.

"The worst thing is," she said, "I don't even know why I called you! I have a midnight flight to the mainland to catch, but instead of grabbing my suitcase and racing out the door, I ran to the phone, looked up your number and called you!"

A bell went off in my mind as she spoke, telling me that what she said had great importance. "Wait a second, Lynette," I said, clearing my head, "Why are you going to the mainland?"

"There is a psychologist there who is so good, I save up my money, and when I can afford the plane fare, I fly over there for a counseling session. Then I go back home to integrate what I learned while I save up some more money."

This psychologist *must* be great, I thought. "Tell me, does this psychologist happen to be in San Diego?"

"Yes," she said with wonder, "but how did you know that? I didn't tell you where he lives!"

"Well," I said, "I'm going to be in San Diego in two weeks, and I just have the strongest feeling that I'm supposed to meet him. Could you give me his name and number?"

The next morning I called the home and office of Dr. Chuck Spezzano. Unbeknownst to me, I was calling during Lynette's session. She and Chuck were just starting back to work after having taken a ten minute break, when the phone rang.

"Lynette," Chuck said with a baffled look on his face, "I've never taken a phone call during a counseling session before, but I have the strongest feeling that I'm supposed to take this call. Would you mind?" She didn't.

When Chuck answered, I explained that I was a friend of Lynette's and that I wanted to have a session with him. I also explained that I would have only one small slot of time free to see him on a day two weeks in the future.

Chuck moaned a little in sympathy, saying, "You know, I travel a lot teaching seminars, and when I'm home my schedule is booked up way in advance. But let me look." After a pause, he said with surprise, "Do you know, just this morning I had a cancellation for that exact time? It turns out I *can* see you!"

Two weeks later I found my way across California freeways to Chuck's home. When he opened the door I was struck by what a lovely man he seemed to be. Handsome, warm, and friendly. As we spoke, I really began to appreciate his professionalism. Any awkwardness I might have experienced in being alone with an attractive (and incidentally unmarried) man in his home was erased. I felt completely comfortable and safe.

The session was quite remarkable. The work he did with me was so deep and so easy, it broke the boundaries and limitations of traditional therapy. They did not teach anything this quick and successful back in graduate school! And interestingly, Chuck's work was based on concepts from *A Course in Miracles.* I had simply never been so impressed with a therapist's work before. It caused me to remember that I had asked Heaven to provide me with a person who had embodied the concepts from the *Course* that I could emulate as a role model.

During our tea break, Chuck left me to go to his office in another part of the house. I later learned that, while he was there, he said a little prayer: "God, if you ever want me to marry," he said with a grin, "I want one like *this!*"

The second half of our session focused on my failing marriage. Chuck used an intuitive method of role playing, in which he "became" me. I, then, could ask myself questions and get answers from a deeper source than my muddled conscious mind.

Usually, Chuck enjoys great success with this method. In my case, however, I was quite surprised to hear him say just how much I really wanted my marriage to work. I had no idea that he felt attracted to me and that he might be making an extra effort to not interfere in my marriage. Mentally, I committed to more marriage counseling back home with my husband.

At the end of the session, I felt moved to make an offer to Chuck. I told him about the Support Center and our training program for volunteers. If I promoted a workshop for him in Honolulu that would cover his expenses, would he donate an evening to training the Support Center volunteer staff? Chuck looked pleased. He had wanted to do some work in Hawaii. We made rough plans to hold the workshop the following August, nine months away.

On the way out, Chuck offered an odd suggestion. He told me of an elderly lady nearby who taught art classes on color therapy and healing mandalas. The woman was also a gifted tarot card reader, and even had an old deck that was given to her by the King of the Gypsies in Europe. She was such a beautiful woman, such a human treasure, that I might want to meet her while I had the chance.

I hesitated for a moment. I had avoided tarot cards all my life out of fear, but this woman certainly sounded benevolent. And what were the odds that she would be free to see me now, with no advance warning, anyway?

Chuck gave me her phone number and I dialed. A sweet voice answered. Yes, of course, she could see me if Chuck recommended it, and she was free now!

Within half an hour I was sitting with her in her art studio in front of a spread of cards. I do not remember much of what she told me, but I do recall that without any prompting she began to tell me about my marriage. "Your husband is a very nice man, but you were never supposed to marry him! There is no deep connection."

With hardly a pause, she continued, "Chuck now, on the other hand...isn't he *wonderful?* He is truly a genius!" I do not know what she saw in the cards, but I had to agree. Chuck was wonderful.

Six months later, after more marriage counseling, my husband and I decided to divorce. We divided up our possessions and filed the paperwork ourselves, not even using a lawyer. It was as amicable as an ending could be, but I still felt like my life had ended. I was a failure, and the future looked bleak and unpromising. I had no idea that the best part of my life was just beginning.

*You may wonder how you ever became isolated
from your emotions in the first place, Sweetheart.
It was, really, unavoidable.*

*You were taught as a child not to talk about your
emotions—and eventually not to even feel them.
Finally you lost the sense that you had the right to
feel what you feel....*

HONESTY

I remember an initial "intake" interview with one of the
Support Center's original families. It was a beautiful Hawaiian day, and I conducted the interview outdoors around a
large low table on the lanai, so that we could enjoy the garden
and the breeze.

The father of the family was Caucasian, the mother
Hawaiian. They were Mormon, and true to their faith, they
had produced five children between the ages of seven years
and six months. The parents were young and obviously in
love. The children seemed well-loved and bonded with their
parents and each other.

It was the second son, David, age five, who was under-
going treatment for leukemia. He had a rather irrepressible
personality–smiling but somewhat conscious of his bald
head. He tussled a bit with his older brother, age seven, as
I seated the parents in chairs. The children sat with us,
kneeling at the table to draw with paper and pastels. I
provided the art materials partly to keep the children enter-
tained, and partly to see, by way of art interpretation, what
they would express in their drawings.

As I gathered information about the family, and what was
going on with little David, I drew a picture too. My picture
was a Hawaiian scene of the ocean and a little island. I put
a blue and green sailboat in the waves, with the sun shining
down on it.

As I talked with the parents, I discovered that they had never discussed with the other children the fact that David had leukemia. They had not wanted to frighten them, so they had never spoken of it openly. I knew that it would be much easier for the children if the problem was out in the open, so they could voice their fears and concerns, express emotion, receive comfort, and straighten out their misconceptions.

I began to explain to the parents that it really would be valuable for them to sit down and explain to the children that David had leukemia, and what that meant; to tell them what the procedures were like for him at the hospital, what his prognosis was, and what they might expect. As I was saying this, David's older brother interrupted once to ask mother, "Mom, how do you spell 'Titanic'?"

I looked at the picture he was drawing. His theme was nautical, like mine, but his boat was large and drawn in heavy dark lines of black and brown and red.

His mother spelled the word for him, and sure enough, he wrote on the side of his boat, "Titanic." As I looked at the picture I could see that the boat was sinking, and that it was on fire. Little figures floated in the ocean, and they had horrible looks on their faces. One out in front looked like a little boy, his hair sticking straight up, and his little mouth drawn in a circle, as if he were saying, "Ooh! Save me!"

When the interview drew to a close, the parents planned a family meeting to discuss David's illness. As they were preparing to leave, I noticed that the brother had completed his drawing. He had placed a blue and green sailboat in the foreground of his picture, near the drowning figure; the boy was being rescued. He would be all right. He would be able to talk about the fear in which he had been drowning.

As the family departed, little David stopped and turned back to me. After only a moment's hesitation, he barreled towards me and caught my legs in a fierce hug. Then he dashed out the door.

You could begin now to feel what is in your heart. You have the support, the permission, and the strength. I am with you in a very real way, Sweetheart. We are all one and there is no separation between us. I know how you feel. I know who you are. Deep inside that's all you really long for...to be known.

The greatest desire of the human heart is to be fully known, and therefore truly loved....

JOHN

While I was working at the Support Center, I took a trip to the neighbor island of Maui to attend a training titled "Life, Death, and Transition." The weekend was a powerful one for me.

As I boarded the plane on Sunday afternoon to fly back to Oahu, I was still caught up in the experience. I sat on the plane in such deep reverie that I did not pay any attention to the other passengers...until someone came and sat beside me that could not be ignored. He was a young man about the age of 20; tall, powerfully built, beautiful, and blond. The most remarkable thing about this young Viking was the exuberance and vitality that beamed from him.

I had to notice him; there was no choice. He fairly scooped me up with his enthusiasm and brilliant pleasure. He told me that he had just competed in a canoe race on Maui. His team had won their heat. It was the first time that he had been steersman, and he had done well. He was on top of the world. He recounted every aspect of that race to me, reliving all of its glory.

When the short flight was over, I realized that I really cared about this boy, that I was thankful that there was one among us who had it all, who could enjoy his life to the fullest, who would receive every good thing that life had to offer. I was happy for him, and wished him the very best when we bid farewell and exited the plane.

Back at my job the next week the psychiatric nurse from the Children's Hospital called me with a new referral. She had a boy in the hospital who was bitter, resentful, and resistant. He was ill with cystic fibrosis, a genetic disease in which the lungs become filled with scar tissue, and eventually stop functioning.

He was miserable and miserable to be around, she said. The nurse did not have high expectations, but she thought that our program might possibly be of help. At least she could rest assured that she had attempted all possible recourse.

She said that, to her great surprise, when she mentioned my name, the boy was willing to see me. This was out of character, but she was not about to question it.

The next morning I went to the hospital and found the patient's room. When I entered it, I could not believe my eyes. Sitting up in bed with an IV hooked to his forearm, sat my big, gorgeous Viking. He wore a grin from ear to ear.

Apparently, he had learned my name on the plane, and recognized it when the nurse had mentioned me. My mind stopped; I was in shock. Grief hit me like a fist in my gut. "How can this be?" I asked him. He told me about his illness, and how he had fought it every step of the way.

The cystic fibrosis had diminished his lung capacity and limited his ability to breathe. He had fought to keep his body as oxygen efficient as possible. He worked out and lifted weights to the point of heroics. Yet the illness pressed on him. The canoe race last weekend had to be his last. That was why winning it had meant so much to him.

People born with severe forms of cystic fibrosis usually die in childhood or in their teens. It was special that he had lived to the ripe old age of 21. What he faced was an uphill battle. Recently he had not been able to deal with the depression of his loss, and he had become angry.

I believe it was the shared experience of his triumph that enabled John to open himself to me. He talked about the things that worried him: What about death? What would happen to him?

I told him everything that I had learned about what happens when we die–the stories people have told of their experiences when brought back from death, the brilliant loving light that beckoned them, the family and friends from the other side who were there to meet them, freedom from all pain.

He wanted me to visit often. We had long talks of philosophy and metaphysics and developed a friendship. He arranged leave from the hospital once to take me to the university to watch a video tape of a Leo Buscaglia lecture on love.

It broke my heart that my fantasy about John would not come true. He was not to "have it all." He would never have his health, a wife or children. That in no way diminished what John did have in abundance: beauty, love, and the courage to steer his course with all his heart.

As you feel tugs of emotion, use them as a life-line to your heart! Use the feelings that emerge as a means to learn how to feel again, to become fully alive!

Open your heart, Sweetheart, and risk to feel! Any emotion, any feeling can be a thread that leads you back into your heart, and then to your inner connection to love. Any time you begin to vibrate with emotion, an opportunity exists for you to release another layer of old pain, heal yourself, and further open yourself to life.

SHANNON

Of all the children that first came to the Support Center, Shannon made his way into my heart the fastest. He was a boy ten years old, of Portuguese extraction. I met him in the hospital the day after his second surgery, an unsuccessful attempt at removing a large and rapidly growing brain tumor.

This surgery had caused nerve damage to the left side of his body. Now that side of him could no longer smile, could not grasp an object. Now, when he walked, he would have to drag his left leg along behind him. His head was shaved; a stitched incision mapped his skull and startled the eye. He was trying to drink through a straw when we were intro-duced. He was still a bit befuddled, and I was told he might not remember my visit.

It struck me that Shannon and his mom were acting "strangely," in that they both seemed free of resistance to what was happening. There was no cloud of tragedy in the hospital room. They seemed to accept what had happened as simply what was. I felt a lot of respect for both of them.

As the weeks went by, Shannon reached right through my shyness and pulled me toward him as a friend. I basked in the fun and closeness of our relationship. When he came to the Support Center meetings, he would limp in wearing dark sunglasses, moving his good hand like an Egyptian, and announce himself as "Joe Cool at the Support Center." Then he would slap me on the ass and say, "Hiya, Lence! How ya doin'?" I loved his style. I was totally smitten.

One day, out of the blue, Shannon converted from Catholicism to become a Southern Baptist, and soon I had the pleasure of witnessing Shannon's baptism. There, after being totally immersed, he popped out of the baptismal pool with a huge grin, and with a wave towards the front of the congregation, sang out, "Hi, Mom!"

When Shannon could no longer attend school, we spent more and more time together. He would hang out with me at my office, or have me over to his house to visit and meet his extended family.

Shannon's condition seemed stable enough. None of us were prepared when he hemorrhaged and died one night at home in his mother's arms. When she called to tell me, I felt the pounding of adrenaline, but no grief.

She asked if I would give the eulogy at Shannon's funeral. I felt touched and honored, and glad for the chance to tell others what I had learned from my little friend. I was puzzled about my lack of emotional response to the loss. Could it be that my metaphysical/spiritual belief in life after death spared me from experiencing grief?

A few mornings later I walked into that same Baptist church, now full of Shannon's family and friends and the big gang of families and volunteers from the Support Center. Love was a tangible bitter-sweet presence that hung in the air and made vision more clear and pristine, somehow. One could sense that all the elements of a great alchemy were brewing, and that there was an opportunity for all of us to be swept up into some sort of great Encounter.

As I sat down a couple of rows behind Shannon's parents, I looked at the order of the service in the program. I was to speak after the congregation sang a hymn. I felt inside myself, assured that I was inspired, on purpose, prepared.

What I was not prepared for was the hymn, Shannon's favorite song. Together we sang "Jesus Loves Me." For many of us adults it was the first time we had sung the song since we had loved it as children.

The power and simplicity of the song leveled us and we became as children again ourselves. It was too sweet, too real, too personal, too poignant. It stripped us of any defense that separated us from our hearts and our feelings. There was no protection from the reality of being at the funeral of a beautiful child whom we each had loved. We all cried our hearts out. And then, all too quickly, the song was over, and it was time for me to speak.

I was completely in the throes of a great wave of emotion. I had lost my ability to focus my attention, to walk to the podium and to speak. Shannon's mom turned around in her pew, her eyes shining. Her look willed me to get up. I could hear her unspoken message: DON'T CRY! She wanted the funeral to be a celebration of Shannon's life.

Using my well-developed ability to suppress my feelings, I felt a powerful internal mechanism reach up from my stomach, take the emotion in my throat into the iron grip of its fist, and then plunge back into its black depths. The door to my grief was once again closed. I told myself that I would open it again later to finish processing my feelings.

I found I was able to walk to the front of the church and speak. My voice was soft, but I did not cry. I said all the things I wanted to say. I shared the lessons of life that Shannon had taught me; gave the gifts that he had given to me. As a group we began to receive inspiration, love, and even happiness.

Afterwards, we all went downstairs to the church hall and had one heck of a great party. The kids were laughing and running around, and the adults were laughing and hugging. It was beautiful. We experienced Heaven in that room. The party lasted for hours. No one wanted to leave.

I went home late that afternoon and thought, "Well, now I can cry. Now I can get it over with." But I just sat there and could not feel anything. The door that had opened so briefly to let out emotion during the hymn was shut tight again. I could not even find a crack or a seam to show me where the door was. My defense mechanism was back in control. It would be another month before that door opened again.

What if your heart were to open right now?
What if you found it full of poignancy and deep
feeling?

What if you let go of all resistance and simply
fell into your well of emotion? Would there ever be
an end to it? Would you ever find your way out?

It is good that you ask, Sweetheart, because it
is a question that you must face, a risk you must
take. And I can answer you confidently:

There are no bottomless wells of emotion inside
you. It is safe to feel any emotion, no matter how
large it may look. Feeling the emotion is what
completes it and heals it. Then, at the emotion's
end, you will find your heart, and you will learn its
function....

LISA

About a month after Shannon died, we had our next crisis at the Support Center. A beautiful young girl named Lisa was due for surgery. She was 15 years old, of Filipino and Portuguese extraction.

Popular and bright, Lisa was a cheerleader at her high school. That's how her cancer was discovered. During a football game she had jumped up to perform a cheer, but when she landed her leg would not support her. X-rays in the emergency room revealed bone cancer in her knee.

When I first met Lisa, her beautiful waist-length hair had already been cut into a short bob in anticipation of the chemotherapy treatments that would ravage her body and make her bald. The first course of chemotherapy was aimed at reducing the size of the tumor in her knee. When the doctors were satisfied with her progress, they would perform surgery to remove her knee. If, when they opened her up, her leg bones were beyond redemption, she would have to lose her entire leg at the hip.

The night before her surgery, I could not imagine the horror of our Lisa, beautiful Lisa, having only one leg. I felt I had to go to the hospital to give her and her family some support, perhaps even encourage them. I certainly could not hide from the task, although I would have liked to. I prepared myself as best I could during the drive to the hospital.

Through the maze of elevators and corridors I found my way to Lisa's room, and finding the door closed, I knocked. I heard muffled voices. Conspiratorially, the door opened just a crack. Black eyes looked out at me. "It's OK, it's Lency," I heard. "You can come in!"

And with a giggle, I was pulled into the room, the door closing quickly behind me. There with Lisa were her grandmother, mother, and sister. They had sneaked in a pizza for Lisa to eat (a no-no before her surgery). Lisa clearly relished the treat, and delighted in their unified declaration of feminine power.

She was sitting on her bed, enjoying every naughty, delicious bite of her meal. I looked around me, completely stunned. I had walked in on a party! These women were laughing, teasing, playing, having fun and enjoying themselves. What I was seeing was impossible!

How could these women have the courage to feel joyful the night before Lisa might lose her leg? How could they conceivably have that horrible possibility (actually a probability) tomorrow, yet have the ability to choose to be happy in this moment? The impact of what I was witnessing brought tears to my eyes.

Lisa's mother, Liz, saw the look on my face and sat me down on the room's other bed. "It's hard, we know," she said as she put her arm around me and patted me.

I looked at them all, dumbfounded. They were comforting *me*. They were encouraging *me*. Fortunately, they carried on with their party, gossiping, joking, laughing, and feeling sentiment. It was not that they were denying their feelings. They were *truly* happy.

After a few minutes, I decided that I had "helped" them enough. I had the good grace to wish them the best, and leave. As soon as I closed the door behind me the emotion hit. The poignancy and power of their commitment to shining the Light of their hearts hit me so hard that I was knocked into my well of feeling; I began to grieve. I grieved for Lisa's lost perfect adolescence. I grieved for her mother's heart.

I grieved for Shannon's death. The loss for his family. The loss of him from my life. The tears streamed down my face, my hands groping to find the button to the elevator. I made it out the hospital doors and through the parking lot to my car. I cried all the way down the freeway–great heaving wails of grief.

Grieving, not for the children any longer, but for myself. Every small but heartbreaking loss. Every disappointment. Every little death that I had stuffed down inside of me and had not had the courage to feel...my own well of grief and disappointment.

As I drove, I thought that I needed to turn the windshield wipers on to be able to see. But it was not raining outside, it was raining inside.

It was the night for my *A Course in Miracles* study group to meet. I drove there blindly, just wanting to reach my friends. When I arrived, late, stumbling up to them at the church where we met, I could speak no words. My face must have said it all.

Every person there got to their feet and went to me, guiding me to their center. They held me there while I grieved and birthed, while I emptied myself of a lifetime of death. Hours later, without ever having exchanged a spoken word, they placed me, still sobbing, in my car. I drove off to find my way to bed, to cry myself to sleep.

When I woke the next day, it was an awakening similar to the one I had experienced in college when I walked away from the counseling center for the last time. It was a day worthy of beginning a new calendar, of measuring my life from that moment on. From this beginning, a new world, a new life, a new heart.

Lisa's surgery went very well. Her kneecap was removed. A temporary metal bar now connected the bottom of her leg to the top. And where there once had been bone, the doctors sprinkled bone chips from her hip. A new bone would grow in its place.

Lisa lived another five years before finally dying of the cancer. She maintained the dignity of her character, her fun sparkle and her love of life even to the end.

Perhaps the most important thing my experiences at the Support Center taught me was how to grieve. It took a month for me to grieve after Shannon's death. With each subsequent death, I was able to grieve sooner, so that finally I was able to let go of a friend as I saw them the last time, and say goodbye in the presence of Love.

I have kept in touch with Lisa's mother through the years. This week, I happened to drop by to see her where she works at the department store in the mall. As always, we were very glad to see each other.

It was as if she stepped right out of her body to join me in an alliance of truth and courage and strength. We were totally real with each other in the presence of our loss, and the joy of being able to feel love.

Not a mushy sort of person, still, she held my hands and said, "You'll never, never know how much you have helped me and how much I appreciate it. If you had not kept after me and got me to the Center, what would have happened to me? If I had not had the support from the Center, and the tools that I learned, there is no way that I could have accepted Lisa's death.

"It's really tough at times because I miss her so much, but I have her friends, and I have Virgie and Norma (other mothers from the Center), and there is so much good happening in our lives. Because of all the love, I have enough Lisa to last me a lifetime."

Human beings are often at their very best when things are worst. To be free of pain at any time, you need only move forward into the light, shining forth the blessings of your heart, contributing to the good.

When you are willing to do this, Sweetheart, you will no longer require pain to learn your needed lessons. The pull of love and happiness will teach you all that you need to know.

A major contribution of miracles is their strength in releasing you from your false sense of isolation, deprivation and lack.

A Course in Miracles, Text, p. 4

WENDY

Another of the outstanding characters at the Support Center was a really rascally person named Wenda. We called her Wendy. Wendy was extraordinary in a lot of ways.

It was extraordinary that she was even alive. It was miraculous that she had reached her twenty-first birthday. She had a rare genetic disorder known as idiopathic hyperalkaline phosphatemia, a disease so horrible and so painful that it's difficult to even begin to imagine what life must have been like for her.

Wendy's head was about the size, but not the shape, of a normal adult head, but her body was only 27 inches long, and weighed only 27 pounds. Her bones grew inward on her, so that her ribs curved in and pierced her internal organs. Her body was deformed in ways that made it difficult to imagine how she could have grown in such a way and still stayed alive.

Although her face was not shaped normally, there was real beauty in it, especially in her eyes. And, once you got to know her, you barely saw her body at all, because she was such a force to be reckoned with. She was a very lively and powerful character.

Feisty, and loving, and compassionate, that girl never complained. She just never complained about the constant pain, even though she had to take dosages of pain killers that would kill a horse. She was hooked up to IV's and oxygen tubes all the time as well, just to survive.

In 1982, at the age of 22, Wendy's doctors decided that there was not much more they could reasonably do for her. They were going to unplug her from the IV, and send her home from the hospital to die; it was cruel to keep her going in the state in which she had to live. They believed that when they unplugged the IV and stopped giving her heart medicine and some other medications, she would just naturally die.

Wendy went home to prepare herself for death. She took tremendous interest in planning her funeral. It was to be the biggest "to-do" and great fun for everyone who would be there. She wanted us to play her favorite rock songs, and she wanted to be dressed up in her white communion dress and veil. She would look like a little bride. This symbolized that, since she could not have a husband in this life, she was going to Heaven to be a bride of Christ. Her ethnic background was Puerto Rican, and she was a strong and faithful Catholic.

Most of all, she wanted to give a message at her funeral: a message to her family, friends, and teachers that would say all the things she wanted said. She asked me to write and deliver the message for her.

Her world consisted of the room she lived in, the hospital bed she never left, the tank of oxygen connected to a tube at her nose, and the thousands of trinkets, key chains and tiny stuffed animals that hung above her, within her vision.

She loved "little" things, things that were small like she was. Each little gift over her bed marked someone's visit, a memory. She could barely move, but she reigned in her little kingdom by wielding a wooden backscratcher that she used to extend her reach.

Every morning it would take a couple of hours for her mother to help her find a comfortable position in which to lie. She had to be moved frequently, but very gently, as her bones were as fragile as birds' wings.

Before she started to dictate her message to me that day, she did something that to me was quite touching. She showed me her body. Normally she was a very modest person, but on this day she wanted me to know about the horrors she lived.

Then she started talking in her tiny little voice. She talked for hours as I took notes, until she had said everything that she wanted to say. Then I went home and put it all together.

This is what Wendy wanted said at her funeral:

"I asked my friend, Lency, to put down my thoughts to be read to you today. She has listened to me talk about my feelings many times, and I know she understands me. I also sense that my brother, Gregory, who passed away two years ago at the age of 17, of the same illness, helped to guide her hand. I've had a difficult life, but a successful one. And I want to share with you the precious things that I have learned.

"I see my life as successful because I feel that I have reached the goal of life, when many people do not, even if they live a very long time. The goal of life is to understand that love is everything.

"A lot of things have happened in my life. It's hard for me to even know where to begin. I do not want to bore you with my troubles, but I want to share with you who I am and what my experience in this life has been.

"I have felt a lot of emotional pain, frustration, and despair in my life, although I tried not to show it. So few people have been able to look past the book's cover, to see who I am inside; to see my intelligence, my maturity and my humor. Because of my size, most people treat me like a baby, as if I do not have any feelings. I want to thank my Dad for always knowing how to treat me.

"I've always wanted a special someone, but most boys have been afraid of me. I've felt a lot of jealousy for my sisters and friends who could go out on dates. I cannot even wear normal clothes and jewelry because of the bones in my chest.

"So many times I felt that nobody understood me. So many nights I cried myself to sleep. So many times I wanted to kill myself. So many times I felt dead inside.

64

"My life has been like a roller coaster, especially these last few years. Many times I wanted off, and many times when I was heading down too far too fast, I was afraid I would fall off. But I always managed to stay on the tracks, taking the ups with the downs. I want to thank my high school teacher, Miss Yamada, for always listening to me, for accepting me, and encouraging me.

"I'm a very independent person. I like to do things for myself. One of my most difficult challenges in life has been my helplessness, my dependency on others. I've always found it disgusting to not be able to do things for myself. I've lived a life without privacy. My mom has had to wash me and dress me every day. It takes hours of her time.

"It hurts me to see that because of me, people get tired. I feel so bad that Mom suffers back pain from lifting me so much, and she's spent countless hours just sitting with me. I know she has suffered a lot. It's as if I've kept her locked up like a prisoner all these years, because I've always wanted her with me. I feel now that I have thrown away the keys to that prison. I want you to know how much I love you, Mom. And how thankful I am for everything you've done for me. I hope you and Dad can start a new life together.

"I've become very tired of living in Wenda's body. Sometimes I could not believe my life could be so difficult, and that I could feel so much pain. If they could make my lungs feel better, my stomach would get upset. And if they got my stomach to settle, my lungs, or head or something else would bug me. It's so hard to sleep at night, and I'm always so afraid of being hurt. It's been so long since I've had a moment's peace without pain.

"I hate feeling always hooked up to something: oxygen and IV, when I just want to be free. And besides hating my body, I sometimes hated myself for not appreciating what people did for me.

65

"My life has not been an easy one. I've never been able to accept my handicaps. I've had many challenges and many disappointments. But I've always known that God has a reason for everything that happens. That reason, the purpose of my life, was shown to me by a very special group of people, my friends from the Young People's Support Center. It is wonderful to have so many beautiful people in our lives now. Before, my family was isolated, but now we're open, and my mom has friends to talk to and lean on.

"I've never had a chance to make many friends. I was always put with the same kids at school, and never had anyone else for a friend. Now I have Lisa and Stephanie, and I cannot believe I can open my heart so wide for them. The volunteers from the Center wrote a book to me, and it was in that book that I found out who I am. I did not see myself as they could see me. I did not understand all that I had done to help other people. I did not realize that God had chosen me to be one of His teachers.

"My belief is that life is like a rainbow. At the beginning we struggle uphill. But at the end, if you make it, you find the pot of gold. I found the gold in all of you here. I found it in true friendship and love. To me, you shine just like gold.

"I found out what God's plan and gift to me was: the ability to help other people. I feel full inside. Love is everything."

Wendy kept this letter in a file, hidden away in her room. Her mother promised that she would not open it until Wendy died. One day, Elisabeth Kubler-Ross (the expert on death and dying) visited. Wendy asked her to pull out the file and read it.

Kubler-Ross was so impressed with Wendy's letter that she had the last two paragraphs of it printed on little calling cards for Wendy. There was a drawing of a pot of gold and a rainbow on the cards. Wendy spent many hours coloring them in. She gave these cards to people who visited her.

Some people were so touched by the gift she gave, that those cards found their way all around the world. The Pope and Mother Theresa each received one. The words were put into a song. Wendy really did touch a lot of people's lives.

I read Wendy's message at her funeral in 1990, eight years after she was sent home to die.

> *I invite you to feel the bitter-sweet throb of your heart. You are present now with your sadness as well as with the love that is flowing into you. Open yourself to the burn of it, open yourself to the tenderness.*
>
> *Follow it inward into the place where the sadness is the strongest. You may notice a tightness in your throat, or another spot in your body: it is only a catch of emotion. Your attention will melt it away, perhaps into tears.*
>
> *Now see if you can feel the feeling even stronger. Surrender yourself into the emotion and fall through it without resistance.*
>
> *Feel the emotion even more powerfully. Allow yourself to sense the origin of the feeling....*
>
> *Let the memories lift up and float out, as you continue to feel even more. Hold your heart as your goal: win yourself back through your courage and your persistence.*
>
> *The very angels in Heaven enfold you, grateful for your willingness. You are loved more than you could ever imagine. Allow yourself to feel it now. You are loved, Sweetheart. You are loved. And love is everything.*

Miracles as such do not matter. The
only thing that matters is their Source,
Which is far beyond evaluation.
A Course in Miracles, Text, p. 1

ELIJAH

Through the Support Center I met a family of Hawaiians who were fascinatingly religious. Their religion was so real for them, and so much the very core of their existence, that no matter what happened in life, no matter what they saw take place, their eyes were always watching God.

They were members of a fundamentalist Christian church which met all day and evening on Sunday, as well as on Wednesday nights. The members of this family were each named after characters in the Old Testament. Their religion was the basis of their self-identity.

The middle child, seven years old, named Elijah, had cancer. When the family first came to the Center, Elijah's body was already wasted by the disease. Although he was active and alert, he was confined to a wheelchair. The family attended the Center's meetings diligently, and were very supportive of the other families. Meanwhile, Elijah's body slowly failed. His weight fell from 62 pounds to 24 pounds at his death.

During the last few months of his life, Elijah began to have the kind of spiritual experiences that dying people often have, in which other dimensions become more accessible. For example, Elijah began to see that when his sister went to sleep at night (they shared a room), her spirit body rose up out of her physical one to go play with her toys. This startled Elijah in the beginning, but he became used to it.

Later Elijah began to have visions of Jesus. Jesus would come into his bedroom and explain to him that in a short time he would be going with Him to Heaven.

68

Frightening at first, these experiences soon became rapturous for Elijah, and he told his parents of the meetings. Of course, to his parents, who loved and trusted Jesus so much, it was both wonderful and horrible to hear.

They were so happy that Elijah had the comfort of visits from Jesus, but the father said, "Son, couldn't you have asked Jesus if maybe He would change His mind and give you more time to be with us?"

Elijah smiled. "No, Dad, no..."

Soon, Elijah's death was imminent. During the final hours of his life, family and friends gathered around him in his home. As he lay there, barely able to move anything but his eyes, he began to look towards the door. As Elijah continued to watch, his eyes opened wider and wider, and happiness shone in his wan face.

Unable to speak, he could not tell anyone what he saw. His parents could see nothing, but they asked Elijah, "Do you see Jesus coming?"

Elijah nodded, and smiled. Yes, he could see Him. And shortly Elijah closed his eyes and he was gone.

The thing that taught me the most was going to Elijah's funeral. I had never had an experience like it. When someone from that church dies, they have a funeral to end all funerals. The congregation stays at the church all day long, and then they have a big feast afterwards. I mean, they really celebrate a death.

It was the first time I had ever been in this type of church. It was quite an experience. When the minister or anyone said anything, every few words or so all the people in the congregation would interject, "Amen!" or, "Praise God!," "Hallelujah!," or "Thank you, Jesus!"

And they did it with such delight. As if in some way they could not contain themselves because they were seeing that much glory, and feeling that much pure joy. It was as if it just burst out of them. I had never been with people who celebrated everything in life the way these people did. They literally praised everything that happened, without censorship.

I will never forget the minister who spoke. He was an old but spry little Hawaiian man. His eulogy went something like this:

"The last time I saw Elijah...Praise God!...It was here at church...Praise the Lord!..I saw him across the church yard...Praise God!...and I saw him come a-runnin'...Amen!... And that boy ran right in front of me...Thank you Jesus!... and right across my beautiful polished shoes...Praise God!... That was a rascally boy...Amen!"

There was absolutely no sense of judgement involved. It was just, you know, that was Elijah. "He was a *rascally* boy!" And that touched me so deeply. It was so completely non-judgmental; I do not know how to put it better.

Finally, the church service was over and we went out to the grave site. In Hawaii, when you go to a funeral, you bring a fresh flower lei. When the coffin is being laid down into the earth, you lay your lei across it, as a form of saying goodbye, of saying "Aloha." It is an incredibly poignant and touching experience, and a good way of saying goodbye. It really invites the people involved to deal with letting go.

As the coffin was being lowered into the earth, Elijah's parents began singing a Hawaiian song of peace and farewell. It was a song that Elijah loved. The lyrics were in Hawaiian, and translated into English they meant:

Aloha -
    May you know
       His peace.
Aloha -
    May He guide
       and keep.
Be faithful,
    be true
       until we too
         shall say Aloha.

Their voices were so strong, so pure, without any catch, without any constriction. They were completely open, with absolutely no resistance in their hearts or their voices about saying goodbye. It was a complete outpouring of love, a complete outpouring of trust. They trusted their God, and His workings, as they said goodbye to their son. The beauty of it was breathtaking.

That family continued to attend the Support Center meetings. The pain of being confronted with all the children that were still alive must have been incredible, but they wanted to continue to support the other families. They had found the courage and the strength in which human beings can be nourished when they trust.

Trust solves all problems. Trust, Sweetheart. Trust the unfolding of your feelings. Trust your healing process. Trust the life that unfolds before you. It is all happening to teach you, to support you and to liberate you. It is beautiful to be human, a vibrant thread in the tapestry of Love.

A miracle is a service. It is the maximal service you can render to another. It is a way of loving your neighbor as yourself. You recognize your own and your neighbor's worth simultaneously.

A Course in Miracles, Text, p. 2

THE HAPPY REVOLUTION

What a joy it is to look back on the last 12 years and see the continuation and growth of the Center (now called HUGS). It has been a different way of "caring" for children faced with the fear that comes with serious illness. It has placed value on the power of the human heart to receive healing through the act of loving and supporting others.

A place was created in the hearts of these children and their families called "The Center." The Center was not a physical place, it was a relationship. It was a party that happened at the Center's meetings and dinners, at baby luaus and birthday parties, at baptisms, in hospital rooms, during home visits, and even at funerals. Wherever two or more of the Center's participants, volunteers, staff or Board of Directors gathered, that non-judgmental, loving relationship was there too. And where there is love like that, there are miracles. People who had felt isolated and afraid now had family who really understood, people with whom they could be themselves.

Once the program was in operation, a happy revolution took place in the hospital wards. Now the kids and the moms all knew each other, visited each other, did errands for each other, played and gossiped and laughed together.

For the first time you could see strange sights like little four year old Erica pushing her IV trolley through the hospital halls on her way to the big kids' ward to visit her friend Wendy who was 21. And when you caught up and saw them in the room together hanging out, they would be having a blast! What pleasure it is for me to see HUGS still alive, still loving, still embracing, and still keeping the vision.

The opportunity to work at the Center evolved and matured me in a way that nothing else could. The opportunity to see human beings at their very best, their most courageous, most kind, most faithful and trusting was a precious experience.

In addition to remembering all of the kids and siblings and moms and dads, I remember the beauty of a dozen volunteers who ran the program with me. I have never seen a group of people operate together with such harmony and appreciation. Every one of us was there because we wanted to learn and grow. The love we had between us was the "happening" that we invited the families into, the catalyst for the joy that took place at the Center's activities.

The secret of that alchemy was a very simple thing: we related to each other on a horizontal basis, as equals. I was the director, because somebody had to do that part of the job; but our ability to see each other as being *the same*, and then extend that "sameness" to include the children and the families is what allowed the miracles of love to happen. No one was "sick," or the wrong race, or too little, or too old, or too different. We just loved each other.

Dr. Jerry Jampolsky, the founder of California's Center for Attitudinal Healing (the first of such programs for kids with life-threatening illnesses), visited one of our meetings. He was in awe of the love that he could see and feel. "Where did you *find* these volunteers?" he asked me. The important factor was that the volunteers had found their hearts.

My work with the Support Center families healed my broken ability to feel. My heart was alive again! I could feel great highs of inspiration, and I could survive great troughs of sadness or depression. I LIVED my life in a way I had never done before, at least not for many, many years.

A lot of the things I teach now are things I learned from the people at "The Center." People from Malaysia to Switzerland have cried with appreciation for what they've learned from stories I tell about Arthur, John, Shannon, Lisa, Wendy, Elijah, and the others.

They are still teaching, still helping us. They still impress their beauty and wisdom on our hearts and souls. After all, we are still in that relationship of love, and we're still having that party.

You would become a joyful person, Sweetheart, if you could acknowledge the blessings that come to you through every relationship that enters your life.

Love may be found in each unfolding circumstance, each encounter, every moment of time.

[Miracles] intercede for your holiness and make your perceptions holy. By placing you beyond the physical laws they raise you into the sphere of celestial order. In this order you *are* perfect.

A Course in Miracles, Text, p. 3

COURTSHIP

A year after I met Chuck, during his second trip to Hawaii to teach a workshop, we began a relationship. He was the most independent creature you can imagine. He had been known to date a half-dozen different women at the same time, preferably in different ports of call.

He was so fearful of commitment that he could not even say the word "m-m-m-m-marriage." A real rogue, and impossibly attractive. He made it clear that if I wanted to be in relationship with him I had to play by his rules—he could not accept responsibility for hurting me (he obviously already carried too much guilt and heartbreak to be able to handle more).

I knew that I had found my "Dreamboat," my True Husband. Unfortunately, most women felt the same way about him, and he was determined not to get caught.

I continued to sponsor Chuck's workshops, bringing him to Hawaii every couple of months. Each time he came out we tried to schedule a jaunt to a neighbor island, and even managed romantic trysts to Tahiti and Cabo San Lucas, Mexico.

During Chuck's visits to Honolulu we always walked from my home on the slopes of Diamond Head, down through Kapiolani Park, to relax and catch some sun at beautiful San Souci Beach. One perfect balmy afternoon, as we walked back home through the park, we witnessed an amazing phenomenon.

Although there was not a cloud in the sky overhead, a fine mist floated in the breeze, apparently coming from clouds over the mountains. Just in front of us a little rainbow about eight feet tall appeared.

Normally, a rainbow retreats as you move toward it, but this little rainbow stayed put. We marvelled at it as we passed under its arc, turning our heads as we did to watch it disappear...but it didn't! It stayed, planted in that spot, reflecting just as brightly as before, even though the sun was now shining behind it–breaking the laws of physics! It stayed merrily in place as we continued on our way for another 20 yards.

Although we had exclaimed surprise and delight at witnessing this unexplainable wonder, we said little to each other as we continued on our way. Both of us had tucked the experience into our hearts. Both of us read it as an omen that held a golden promise of magic for our future, and foretold of "connectedness" to come.

One morning, during one of Chuck's visits, the ultimate sexual experience happened for me. We had just returned from an early Breakfast Club meeting at which Chuck had spoken. His talk had been especially inspiring, his beauty rendering me rather breathless. When we arrived home, we began to make love.

Then something happened inside me that had never happened before. I think it was because I was in such a state of inspiration and love, that while we were making love, a spontaneous expression welled up from deep inside me. The word that took me over and filled my mind was *welcome*. WELCOME!

I had never welcomed anyone into me that way before. It was emotional, physical, spiritual, and sexual. I was welcoming Chuck into me without reservation, without grievance, without any desire for separation. At the points of our emotional and physical contact, I was totally soft, relaxed, inviting and receptive. It was a transfiguring, glorious experience.

Then I began to have a vision. I could no longer see Chuck, but instead saw a great arcing ray of light/matter extend from me on into infinity. Where it connected with me it was small. As I looked up, this ray of what appeared to be super-brilliant gold and pink clouds extended up ahead of me until it filled the horizon.

I knew that there was no end to it. I knew that I was looking into infinity. And I also knew that I was looking at the face of God, because that Light was looking back at me!

Although I did not see any eyes I knew that I was being seen, and that I was completely loved, and completely known. Perhaps the most profound aspect of the experience was that this Great Intelligence viewed me with a tremendous sense of humor, and lovingly laughed into me with compassion and bliss.

Here was not only something that I would certainly call God (that fit all the classic descriptions like omnipotent and omnipresent and omniscient), but a God that knew me personally, knew absolutely everything about me, loved absolutely everything about me, and thought everything about me was funny—a real hoot!

The most unbelievable part of it all was that this "Godness" led right into me. I mean, in fact it was me. I seemed to be a narrow extension of this Brilliance, as if, as a human being, I was an expression of the very frontier of God.

I hung suspended in the glory of the vision for a time... was it three seconds? Three minutes? It was impossible to tell. And then the vision ended in ecstasy. I started to cry from the impact of it, and for the loss of it. Chuck held me as I cried for hours.

The joy that comes from union with the Divine is more than you are imagining, Sweetheart. Your ability to find God depends on your willingness to see beauty in those around you. Through your expanding capacity to know Heaven's Love, you learn of your own value by reflection.

All miracles mean life, and God is the Giver of Life. His Voice will direct you very specifically. You will be told all you need to know.

A Course in Miracles, Text, p. 1

THE FRAGRANCE OF MAILE

In each of our lives there are amazing events which take place. In 1983 I was blessed with an incredible experience, probably the highest point of my life so far. I was, for the period of a week, lifted into a high level of consciousness; enlightenment, if you will. It is impossible to express what the experience was like, but there were three qualities to it that I will try my best to describe.

The first was an experience of heightened awareness of the present moment. It was a "thought-less awareness," in which my mind still had the ability to think, but was completely free of my usual mental chatter. My mind was relaxed, calm, empty, and full of peace; it was an amazing relief!

My awareness focused on two things. The first was an experience of a golden column of Intelligence that came down through the top of my head into the very core of my being. From this presence came a Voice.

Any time I felt curiosity about anything, the Voice would respond. I had the sense that It had complete access to all the information and wisdom in the universe. It was deeply satisfying to have such communion with Divinity.

The other awareness I had was of my heart. It produced a perpetual soft sweetness, that *felt* the way maile leaves *smell*. (Maile leaves are used to make the most precious of all Hawaiian leis.)

I spent my days feeling the fragrance in my heart, and communicating with the Voice of God. It was Heaven on

Earth. I was able to walk and talk and work and carry out all the tasks of life, but I was freed from the torture of thought. I needed to do nothing but float in the beauty.

Three events led me into this wonderful state. The first was when Chuck and I joined our minds in a common goal. We had come across a potent passage from *A Course in Miracles* which read:

> The peace of God is everything I want.
> The peace of God is my one goal; the aim
> Of all my living here, the end I seek,
> My purpose and my function and my life,
> While I abide where I am not at home.
> (Workbook, p. 380)

We knew that this was what we both wanted; we wanted our relationship to become a Holy Relationship. We wanted one that would transcend "specialness" and needs, to create true love and wholeness, one that would take us all the way Home.

We held hands, looked in each other's eyes, asked Heaven's help and made that commitment. It appears that this commitment set in motion some interesting effects.

The second event was something a friend said to me a couple of evenings before the enlightenment occurred. Chuck and I had visited her and her husband for dinner, and as she and I were cleaning up the kitchen afterwards, I complained to her that it was hard to have to share Chuck with other women.

After hearing what I had to say, my friend laughed and said, "Obviously, the only way out of pain in this situation is to heal! You wanted to heal your ego anyway, didn't you? Use this opportunity to do just that!"

Her words really struck me. Of course she was right; I did want to heal my ego! As Chuck and I drove back to my place, I made a commitment to him.

I decided that regardless of what form our relationship would take, I was committed to being in relationship with him as a friend forever. Whether he would be my lover or not, I would always love him. Nothing but my support for him was really important. I felt a shift take place in the way I saw him that was very liberating.

The third event took place in Chuck's workshop two days later. A lady there raised her hand and spoke of a serious problem she'd had most of her life.

Instead of approaching the woman's problem with one of his ever-successful methods, Chuck intuitively stated that I had the answer for her. He suggested that I "get in touch" with my Higher Self so that I could then discover what to do.

I had never done anything like that before, but my trust in Chuck was so complete that I easily slipped into a meditative state and accomplished what he asked. Soon I was empathically describing what this woman's life had been like. It was a painful story to hear, and as I spoke, the woman began sobbing uncontrollably.

Then a sense of power and exhilaration came through me and I asked her if she would like me to take the problem out of her? "Yes!" she cried. "Are you sure?" "Yes!" she answered.

I walked over to where she was sitting, reached toward her upper chest, and pulled something not physical but entirely tangible out of her, and threw it away from us. She shrieked as I did so, and cried out to the others, "It's true, it's true! It really happened! It's real!"

I instructed the people there to surround her and place their hands on her. As we did this I felt the meditative state deepen into the experience of enlightenment that I described earlier.

I floated in an astounding sense of peace. I assumed that to maintain it I would have to hold completely still. I could not imagine moving my body and being able to perpetuate the feeling.

I eventually found that I could not only move and still feel it, I could stand, and walk and even talk, and the state did not dissipate. This was unbelievably wonderful! Everything looked different from this vantage point.

I remember telling Chuck that if women made him happy, he should have lots of them! I was not attached, did not need to own him; I was too content in the bliss I was feeling to need to change or control him.

I loved him in a greater way than I had before. I was more open-hearted. Sex was *great*. I felt a degree of partnership with him that was beyond anything I had ever imagined; a holy relationship.

By the end of the week, I had begun at times to drift out of the enlightened state. I would discover myself beginning to think. When this happened I remembered to turn my mind over to the Voice to plan the day and do the thinking, and remembered to turn my attention over to the sweetness in my heart.

I realized that making this simple choice is what life is all about: learning to remember to let God run the show while we pay attention to the love. And I realized that it is always that easy to feel love—we just have to have the willingness to move our awareness to the place where we can receive it.

Then, unfortunately, in a phone conversation with Chuck (he was now back on the mainland), I realized that he did not trust that the openhanded way I was treating him would last. It was difficult for him to believe the vision I had of our partnership. Given his past this was understandable, but to me it was devastating. If Chuck could not join me here, said the temptation, I had better go after him!

And then I fell, a long agonizing tumble into darkness and pain; a fall like the original fall, and the others like it that I had experienced throughout my life. They were all bad, but this was one of the most crushing because I fell from so high a place and landed much lower than where I had begun a week before.

It was horrible to begin the slow struggle back uphill, feeling so dense, self-centered and full of ego, knowing all the work that would have to be done to regain myself. I was heartbroken, but at least I had learned what lies ahead for us if we are willing to open our hearts. I knew the direction in which our happiness waits, and I began to move once again along that path.

All of us are seeking to find God, whether blindly or with constant desire and attention. Let yourself not be distracted, Sweetheart. To be in communion with Heaven is the purpose of existence.

Each day should be devoted to miracles. The purpose of time is to enable you to learn how to use time constructively. It is thus a teaching device and a means to an end. Time will cease when it is no longer useful in facilitating learning.

A Course in Miracles, Text, p. 2

FEEL EVERYTHING

Keeping a connection with the Center by serving on its Board of Directors, I left its employ to become an instructor in the Transformational School that Chuck, another psychologist (the friend who gave such good advice), and I put together.

Chuck moved to Hawaii, and we rented a house together in a lovely neighborhood that had been carved out of a banana plantation on the Windward side of Oahu. The lush trees and tropical gardens set in the frame of the dramatically sheer cliffs of the Koolau Mountains and babbling mountain streams were my idea of paradise. When it rained we could see six waterfalls thread their way down the valley walls, and at night the sky was blanketed with stars.

Around this time an interesting thing began to take place. A new gift was beginning to emerge in my heart.

Chuck was a very busy man. In addition to instructing at the Transformational School, he had been drafted to be the minister of Windward Unity Church (the church members were so in love with Chuck that they had him ordained), and he kept up his international work as a seminar leader.

At the church I held the unenviable position of being the minister's live-in girlfriend. This was an uncomfortable role for me, not because of any eyebrow raising or judgement (the

84

congregation was too hip for that), but because so many of the members had a secret, or not so secret, crush on Chuck.

Having only "girlfriend of the minister" status, standing with Chuck in the reception line after the church services for handshakes and hugs was out of the question. After the first couple of months, however, I noticed that I had developed my own reception line outside by the refreshment table.

Every week this long line of people would queue up, patiently waiting for me to embrace them. As I held each one I would begin to feel things. Sometimes sadness, sometimes hurt or shame. Often the other person, or I, or both of us cried briefly, until we felt a happiness. Then the person would thank me, brightly, saying, "I just had to have my hug!" Or, "I wouldn't miss my weekly hug!" It was a strange phenomenon, even somewhat embarrassing. What was happening?

It seemed as if I was beginning to be able to feel what other people were feeling. I was extremely confused about it all at first, because people sometimes denied feeling what I experienced them to feel.

For instance, Chuck and I happened upon a friend in a restaurant one day. She informed us that she had just sold her house and would be moving into a condominium. As she spoke, I could feel a tremendous wave of sadness and loss. I responded by saying that it must be very sad for her to leave her dream house. She answered, "Nonsense, I don't feel that way at all. The house needed a lot of repair and it will be much easier to live in the condo."

As she spoke, I continued to feel the grief. I was totally confused, and commented on it to Chuck as we left the restaurant. "Are you kidding?" he answered. "Don't you realize how much she is in denial of her feelings? If I were you, I wouldn't discredit my experience purely on the strength of what another person *reports* to be feeling."

And so I studied the phenomenon. As my experience with it grew, I came to the conclusion that I could indeed, at least at times, feel what other people were feeling. I just did not know if this was the good news, or the bad news.

I considered the question seriously. It seemed that the feelings came when I *empathized* with others, when I cared about them and how they were feeling. It also seemed that good came from these connections, these happenings. People were helped, because healing was the product of the joining.

What would happen to *me* if I continued to feel all of these feelings? I wondered. Would this "becoming one" with other people damage my body or psyche in some way? If I completely let go, threw caution to the wind, and felt everything that I could feel, would I go insane? Would I die?

I felt frightened. I could not find any material in the literature about this kind of work. I could not find any teachings or spiritual paths related to feeling your feelings–I do not know if there were any written at that time. My heart told me that I was on *my* path, and that I needed to follow it.

Finally, it was knowing Chuck that helped me make the decision. I reasoned that if I did surrender into the realm of emotion, and somehow became lost there, that Chuck would be able to find me and bring me back.

So I decided to feel everything that I could feel, whether it seemed solely my own emotion, or an experience I shared with another person. Deep in my mind I believed that it benefited me as much as anyone that I seemed to help.

I developed a private therapy practice, in which I not only counseled, but joined with my clients to produce emotional healing. With their ability to feel restored, they resolved relationship and health problems, and became free of old recurring issues.

I began teaching seminars with Chuck using my concepts and methods, and I learned how to work with the hearts and minds of a whole group of people at the same time. It seemed that by empathically opening myself to feel the pain of others, my own old pain was released.

I discovered that there were no bottomless pits of emotion–just buckets of it that could be emptied. It was safe to let go and fly through emotion as rapidly as possible so that it finished quickly.

At one point I made a wise request of my Higher Mind. Recognizing that everything that happened in my life took place in order to help me grow, to get me in touch with myself, and to reveal denied and buried places in my mind, I asked for a bargain:

If I was willing to feel everything I could feel in myself and everything I could feel in the people who came to me, would my Higher Mind, or Whoever was running this show, send me the perfect clients to heal *myself?* Could people who had old pain similar to mine bring their problems to me, so that I could use their problems and their trauma to help me get in touch with my own old emotion? We could be healed together, and I would not need as much drama in my life anymore to bring up my "stuff."

Apparently my Higher Mind agreed. From that point on, life did smooth out for me a great deal. I was well rewarded for my willingness to feel. As this empathic healing capability matured, I would learn how to join with others and acknowledge pain, without having to pull all of the emotion through my own physical system. More subtle, elegant and helpful pathways would open and develop.

Accept each day as a call for compassion. Awaken to the needs of those around you, responding with increasing devotion to the healing of separation.

There is only One of us here... as you use your ability to improve conditions for any part of life, all of life is blessed.

Miracles are healing because they
supply a lack; they are performed by
those who temporarily have more for
those who temporarily have less.
A Course in Miracles, Text, p. 1

THE CONFERENCE

When I was first experimenting with the ability to join
with others, I had an experience in which I could use the
expression, "I didn't know my own strength!" Chuck and I
were sponsoring a local Hawaii conference in conjunction
with the annual International Human Unity Conference. We
invited speakers from Hawaii and California to give presen-
tations to the entire conference assembly, and/or to give
smaller group workshops from which the attendees could
choose. In this way, many speakers would have the opportunity to conduct workshops, although not so many would
have the opportunity to address the entire assembly.

The conference unfolded beautifully. The weekend was
a real celebration, full of inspiration, love, and humor. Chuck
was so wide open that he cried through his talk. Our friend,
Terry McBride, was at his shining best. The workshops were
stimulating. Everything was going great.

It turned out that, for some reason, there was one slot of
time left open on the last day of the conference. I was given
that time to do whatever I wanted. I thought, well, there were
a few really beautiful people that the whole group should
have a chance to experience.

And, I thought, it would be great for everyone for these
people to have a chance to give something to the whole
group. So I thought of a couple of people out in the audience
that I wanted to bring up on stage to talk to, and hopefully,
just create a "happening."

I had only recently been developing the ability to join with others. I did not know exactly what would happen if I joined my heart with someone while we were on stage, but I figured something good would come of it.

I had heard that one man, a holistic dentist from California, was having a rough time. He had been fussing and complaining. I felt he was a lovely man doing good work, who could do with some extra support and appreciation.

I got up and announced that there were a couple of people that I wanted to pull up on stage to recognize, in order to give everyone the gift of being able to experience them. When I called the dentist's name, his face showed complete shock. He could not believe what I had said.

With a kind of dazed look he got up, and climbed up on stage as everyone applauded him. I sat him down in a chair, and I said, "We just want to get to know you. We'd like to know more about you, and your wonderful work. What can you tell us about yourself?"

And then I connected up with him. Within moments he burst into tears. He said, "I have been feeling so righteous, and separate. I've been attacking everybody. I'd come all the way from California, and nobody had recognized me. Nobody applauded me, and nobody recognized that I should be up addressing the whole group. Ever since I've been here I've acted small and petty, spreading bad feeling about this to everybody I've come in contact with."

He said all of this through a torrent of tears. He had ripped himself open and revealed his deep, hidden and shameful inner reality. He cried from the joy of being recognized and being loved, even though he had been unloving since arriving.

Then he told us a little story: "When I received the invitation to be a presenter at this conference, I could not decide whether to come. Since there was no offer to pay my expenses I couldn't decide if it would be worth it to come out.

"Finally, I decided that if I could help even one person by attending the conference, I would go, and I booked my ticket. I had no idea at the time that the one person I would be helping would be me!"

He actually helped all of us there. For me and for many others it was the crowning experience of the whole conference. When anyone is healed, he or she is not healed alone.

Each soul chooses a unique path of development in life, greatly determined by the mistakes made along the way. Failures teach you and advance you with great speed if you do not resist them.

Recognize and accept your failures, Sweetheart, so that you may progress with ease through your adventure!

> A miracle is never lost. It may touch
> people you have not even met, and
> produce undreamed of changes in
> situations of which you are not even
> aware.
>
> *A Course in Miracles*, Text, p. 4

SMALL ACTS OF KINDNESS

Wouldn't it be wonderful to be able to see the effects of our actions? If we could see the rippling impact they have upon the world and the people around us? Sometimes we would be chagrined to see what we have created. In many other cases, we would be touched to see the effects of even our smallest acts of kindness.

I remember the first workshop I taught on metaphysical healing, which I presented at that Human Unity Conference. With so many other workshops going on at the same time to choose from, I was nervous to see if anyone would come to mine.

I attempted to look casual as the room began to fill. A young man came up and asked if he could speak with me. He began to tell me of a day three or four years before when he and a group of concerned citizens went to Honolulu Hale (the City and County of Honolulu office building) to see Mayor Frank Fasi.

He and his group had to wait while the mayor finished visiting with some deaf people. (They had come to witness the signing of a bill proclaiming the month of May to be Deaf Awareness Month.) The deaf people were excited to be there.

Intrigued by this unusual sight, the young man watched the deaf people interacting with the mayor. As he watched the communication pass from the deaf people to the interpreter, to the mayor, back to the interpreter, and back to the deaf people again, he was struck by the vision of rapport created by the interpreter, and the grace which embraced the group and seemed to fill the room.

The young man had never witnessed that level of connectedness, where the hearts and minds of people were so intimately entwined. The beauty of it inspired him. He told me that hardly a day had passed since that time that he did not recall to mind that picture of "oneness." Of all the human encounters he had witnessed in his life, that one gave him the most hope. When he saw me on the stage with the dentist, he recognized me as having been one of the members of that group, the interpreter. He thanked me for being one of his teachers.

My workshop that day went well enough, although certainly no one has ever told me that it changed their life. Looking back, I was probably self-conscious, my attention as much on my fear as on the people in the room. I may have taught more about being truly helpful that day at the mayor's office in one small act of kindness than I did at the workshop, trying my best to be a teacher.

Many times in my life I have set myself up to be a Helper, or a Teacher, or a Giver of Advice, only to have things turn sour because my motivations were wrong. We are more truly helpful through small acts of kindness and connectedness than we are through our attempts to correct and change those around us.

With every word you speak, and through every action, you teach. Yet it is not always what you think you are teaching that you teach. It is not always what you say that speaks the most loudly.

You are Heaven's teacher, Sweetheart, and the lessons you teach are the lessons you learn. Your acts of kindness, empathy, and compassion touch many, and teach you of your own beauty.

Miracles represent freedom from fear.
"Atoning" means "undoing." The
undoing of fear is an essential part of
the Atonement value of miracles.
A Course in Miracles, Text, p. 2

CHOOSING

Even when Chuck and I were living together, he still
maintained a girlfriend on the mainland whom he visited.
This form of relationship was all he was offering, and I took
whatever I could get.

One day, right before he left to teach a seminar in
Vancouver (a trip on which his other girlfriend would join
him), he said something unusual to me. He said that if there
was anything I could do to make him choose me, I had his
permission.

I knew from past experience that there is inside me (as
there is in all of us), an ability to have anything that I want.
It is an ability that has to do with opening up to receive my
heart's desire. I wondered if I had the courage to actually use
that ability now.

I had never attempted to influence our relationship this
way for fear of reaping bad karma from manipulating other
people's lives. Yet Chuck had invited me to do what I could,
if indeed I could do anything.

Right after Chuck flew off to Canada, one of his best
friends, Terry, arrived on a visit from the mainland. It was one
of those interesting mix-ups. With Chuck off on his trip, off
with his old girlfriend, I began to feel pretty sorry for myself.
Having Terry so available to hear *my* side of things was a
temptation I could not pass up. So one evening after dinner,
as we sat by the pool in our backyard, I told him my story.

It was a story of heroic, long-suffering patience and goodness on my part. Chuck was a charming, but unfeeling, cad. His departure into the sunset, flying off into another woman's arms, was the perfect and poignantly dramatic climax to the sad tale.

As I finished my story, the evening had turned to night. All I could see of Terry was his shining teeth. He was smiling. I waited for a response. Terry chuckled, and said in his most lovable and enthusiastic voice, "All I can say is, for Chuck's sake, I sure hope you choose him!"

After a pregnant pause, I assumed that Terry must not have understood my story. Perhaps he had not been listening too carefully. So I took the next half hour to retell the story. Embellishing it. Adding even more gruesome details of my suffering (and, of course, my goodness and patience).

Once again, when the story was finished, and I looked to him for response, all I could see through the darkness was those big, bright, beautiful teeth: he was still grinning.

He leaned forward and said, as distinctly and intently as he could, "All I can say is, for Chuck's sake, I sure hope you choose him!" And with that, he gave me a kiss on the cheek and went to bed.

Wait a minute. Hold on here! OK. I was generous enough to look at the possibility that maybe Terry was not insane, and that there was, in fact, another way for me to look at this whole situation. What if it truly was a matter of choice? My choice?

Was I ready to have Chuck? Willing for him to be mine? Willing for him to be my husband, my lifetime partner? No other husband, no other lover, no other body, no other romance? Just Chuck, my Dreamboat? The best man in the whole world?

I conceived that what Terry was saying was true. Of course; it made sense. It lined up with my previous experience: I could have anything I wanted. And of course I wanted

Chuck. Why, then, did I feel this incredible fear? It became obvious that my own fear of commitment, even to the most perfect man in the world, was what had stood between me and having what I thought I wanted.

I was a person who had chosen an elusive man because I was afraid of marriage. I was just as elusive. And my "competitor" for Chuck's attention was no more willing to receive him than I!

I had been trying to change the form of our relationship by changing Chuck, but I would have no success until I "got real" and faced my fear. By telling the truth, and moving into the feeling, I could finish it and choose again.

I could have Chuck if I was not afraid to have him. He would be mine if I could get through my fear. What did I want? In very little time I decided that I did want him. I wanted him as my partner, I wanted him as my husband. I wanted him more than I wanted to avoid my fear. And so I chose him!

When I made the choice, I opened up a door to an enormous fear that I had never known existed. I walked through that fear for three days straight. It was solid, continuous, brilliant, strong. It was phenomenal. It was breathtaking. I kept moving through it until, finally, I stepped into freedom.

The fear was over, and all I could feel was the assurance of commitment! I had chosen Chuck, and without speaking with him, I somehow knew that he had chosen me, too.

When Terry drove me to the airport to pick Chuck up, I could not wait to see him. I was so excited!

As it happened, Chuck's flight had arrived early, and he was already off the plane before we made it to the gate. When he spotted us coming down the concourse, a huge grin broke out on his face. With total abandon he ran to me with out-stretched arms! (And this was the man who never showed me affection for fear of leading me on!)

At exactly the time I had chosen Chuck, he had chosen me. It was no coincidence. We were married later that year. Terry was Chuck's best man at the wedding.

When you exercise your courage to face your fears, joy and success will be your companions.
When you are in contact with the center of your being, abundance and blessings are certain to follow.

Miracles restore the mind to its full-
ness. By atoning for lack they establish perfect protection. The spirit's
strength leaves no room for intru-
sions.

A Course in Miracles, Text, p. 3

TRUST

Before our first child, Christopher, was born, our pediatrician warned us about becoming parents. He told us that
from this point on, our lives would no longer be our own.
They would be dictated by something more important to us,
the life of our child, and we would be vulnerable to the world
in a way we never had been before.

In addition to having a clientele of normal, healthy
children, this doctor also carried the largest case load of
pediatric oncology patients in the state of Hawaii. In other
words, he was the cancer specialist for children.

He had seen several hundred families deal with the crisis
of a child with cancer. A profound thing he had learned in
these many years was that it was impossible for a parent not
to love their child unconditionally. He said it did not matter
how it looked, whether the parents were warm or gruff,
seemed smothering or distant; when it came right down to it,
there was not a parent he had ever met that would not have
instantly traded places with their child when the diagnosis of
cancer was given. Not one parent would not have chosen to
suffer or die in their child's place.

Those who are parents know the truth of that statement.
It is impossible to have a child and not love him or her, not
care. Regardless of any appearance to the contrary, that truth

is the bottom line. It takes great wisdom to realize that our own parents have always loved us this deeply.

When Christopher was five weeks old, he required surgery to repair a hernia. The surgery itself was not especially complicated or dangerous, but the fact that he would have to undergo general anesthesia at his age made the surgery more serious. It felt very dangerous and frightening to both Chuck and me. We were afraid that we could lose Christopher. Yet he was in such agony that we knew that we had to do everything we could to try to help him.

The day before the surgery, we were beside ourselves with fear. It was a busy time, with relatives arriving from thousands of miles away for Christopher's christening, and Chuck and I were separated for most of the day. As I ruminated on our situation with Christopher, I came to one conclusion. I realized that the only way for me to feel safe, for Christopher to be safe, was for me to stop fighting with my fear.

I sensed that it was my own fear that was attracting danger to the situation. For the situation to heal, I knew I had to heal the fear that was inside me. I had learned that a good way to heal fear was to surrender into feeling it–to feel it fully, to allow it, to know it–thereby letting it release. Not to go into a panic, but to feel the fear with the goal of completing it.

I chewed on the emotion all through the day. And by evening, I had let Christopher go. I had made peace with the idea that perhaps I had been given this baby for only five weeks.

When this was accomplished, a tremendous change came over me. I had lost my resistance to the surgery, and in its place I felt a confidence and a sense of safety. I knew the outcome would be fine. Excellent, in fact. There was nothing for us to worry about; only good would come of the experience.

When I finally saw Chuck that evening, his face wore the same expression as mine. He had gone through a similar process during his busy day, and was enjoying the same relief. We laughed when we looked at each other, then together turned to the job of comforting and assuaging the fears of our family. The surgery the next day went well. The christening was a joyous celebration.

Whenever you are frightened, Sweetheart, remember that the process of transformation is under way. Nothing that happens to you is random. Everything that occurs is an opportunity for growth, supporting in some way your greater life goal.

> Miracles occur naturally as expressions of love. The real miracle is the love that inspires them. In this sense everything that comes from love is a miracle.
>
> *A Course in Miracles*, Text, p. 1

CHILDREN

I believe that despite all the techniques, trainings, course work, and studying I have done in the area of personal growth, the one thing that has done the most to develop me, to mature me–and that has helped the most in my own evolution–is the experience of becoming a parent. Nothing else has had such influence over me.

Becoming a mother was a rude awakening for me, a terrible shock. It was difficult for me to make the internal adjustments necessary for me to truly parent. I was much too firmly ensconced in the center of my world to easily move aside for a baby to take over.

Not only did having children make me grow up, my kids actually taught me how to do my life's work. Christopher gave me daily, hourly, practice in empathic joining.

As a baby he was a very light sleeper. He also had difficulty falling asleep. And once he did fall asleep on your shoulder, he would awake if he were laid down. At one point he was being held about 20 hours a day (at times like this it's wonderful to not be a single parent!).

I discovered that Christopher fell asleep easier if I consciously moved into his heart with my awareness. I also learned that if I was joined with him I could lay him down, break physical contact and leave the room without his waking.

All he needed was Momma connected to his heart for him to feel safe enough to relax. We were so much a single system that if we were both asleep, and he woke up and opened his eyes, my eyes opened too.

By graduating from Christopher's boot camp, I learned how bonding is accomplished. Since most of our mothers could not provide us with "bondedness" (because their own mothers had not bonded with them), most of us do not have the "wiring" necessary to experience higher emotions like love and bliss.

I have discovered that this "rewiring" or bonding is easy enough to accomplish in a private session or a workshop setting. People have a great hunger for it; it's what we have all been waiting for since birth.

Christopher also helped me develop my ability to join others at a distance. Even with someone on the other side of the planet, I can feel their heart, feel their feelings, as easily as if they were sitting in front of me, or as easily as if they were my baby, asleep in another room.

It seems I can feel anyone I think of or am told about, which is wonderful because, if I can connect with them, I can send them love. Which brings me to the lesson I was taught by my daughter, J'aime.

Many people have loved me throughout my life, but I was 34 years old the first time I felt love flow into me from another human being. It happened one day while I was nursing J'aime, when she was about 6 months old.

As I nursed her that afternoon, and looked into her eyes, I had the experience of a wave of love washing from her to me and into me. For several minutes I luxuriated in the sweetest, warmest, and most powerfully precious emotion I'd ever known with another person.

And as I received her love, I began to understand that the experience was not extraordinary. It was the experience that human beings are made for. A mother and child are designed for sharing this kind of love.

I realized also that this love must be available in every human relationship; this opportunity waited for me with

101

everyone that I knew. It was, perhaps, the purpose of our life on earth. Not love as an idea or a value, but as a feeling that could be physically experienced in our hearts. I recognized that not everyone was able, in their current state, to feel love–to give it, or to receive it.

As I still sat there, nursing J'aime, I wondered if I could feel love that anyone else had for me. I thought I would try it out. The person's name who jumped into my mind, I suppose because he is famous for his teachings about love, was Jesus. "Why not?" I thought.

I intuitively "tuned in" to Jesus and opened myself up to receive from him. Immediately I was flooded with rich, joyful, personal love. All I could think of at the time was, "Wow, what a great guy! So *this* is what Christianity is all about."

These experiences launched me into a quest to discover how to be able to feel love more often, as much as possible. I wanted to share this love with people in a way in which they could actually feel the pleasure of it, the awakening of it. I wanted to let other people know that this love is available, that it is real, that it has substance, and that it has value beyond expression.

Believe in love, Sweetheart. Dare to love. Put your faith in its power, and offer it to the world. Transform every moment into its quest.

Love dearly, love undauntingly, love with all your heart, for love is what you are.

> Miracles are natural signs of forgiveness. Through miracles you accept God's forgiveness by extending it to others.
>
> *A Course in Miracles*, Text, p. 2

TO SEE ONLY BEAUTY

When I see something in someone else that I judge to be wrong, I know that I have an unconscious battle going on with that same trait. I have a hidden, guilty belief that I am that way.

As I take my negative projection off of the other person, and look for the trait in myself, I give it permission to enter my awareness, and I begin to feel it. Soon its presence is welling up and pouring out, and I can remember times when I have acted out the trait (acting just like the person I had been judging). A short time later the emotion is released and I am free of it, healthier and wiser. I can give an example of how I began to look to my inner world to heal disruption and upset in my outer world.

Several years ago, while Chuck was away on a trip, an old friend from college was in the Islands and wanted to see me. Although I felt a strong affection for him, I realized I was also afraid to see him. He held very strong religious views that I did not share, and our last visit some eight years earlier had primarily consisted of locking horns with each other.

I did not want to fight, but I also did not want to hide who I was from him. I was afraid of being judged, of being called a sinner, of being told I was going to hell.

We had dinner and a pleasant visit, but then, when the babies were in bed, we started to really talk. Within minutes, we were locking horns again. I thought I was trying to bridge our two belief systems, but it became obvious to me many hours later that I was only engaged in a struggle to be more "right" than he was.

When I realized what I was doing, I apologized to him for my desire to fight and for my lack of willingness to get closer to him. I shared my feelings of failure and disappointment in my lack of ability to be on the same side with him. I told him that I was dealing with old hurts and pain that had more to do with my past than the present, and that I did not know yet just what it was all about. I told him how I had wanted him to behave and apologized for trying to change him. We recovered our friendship, although much was yet unresolved.

When he left, I began to work on the experience. The first thing I dealt with was my immediate emotion. When I let it have full rein, I felt strong feelings that fit with experiences ranging back to my adolescent and university years: alienation, loneliness, fear of being different, fear of being judged and rejected, and a great desire to please.

I stayed with those feelings until they were exhausted. My reward was a wonderful sense of personal power–power that I had previously given away in my attempts to not cause concern to fundamentalist Christians like my parents.

The next thing I did was begin an examination of my projections on my friend. I had been judging him to be provincial, narrow-minded, inflexible, frightened of change, moralistic, judgmental, opinionated, argumentative, and blind to himself.

Owning these traits as my own was a bitter pill to swallow. As I took my blinders off, I could see just how much I was really exactly the kind of person I was accusing my friend of being! I could picture conversations with other friends in which I acted much like the fellow I had judged. It was pretty embarrassing to see, so I then went ahead and felt the embarrassment, too.

The next angle I took in my efforts to learn from the experience was at the level of what I saw him doing. I applied a concept I learned from Chuck: Anything that I saw my friend doing to me, I must also have been doing to him. Here was another big piece to chew on. I saw him judging me. To him I appeared deluded, wrong, sinful and dangerous. The psychological equation said that, therefore, I must be judging him and his beliefs in the same way.

When I looked inside myself, I was surprised to find just how much judgement and scorn I felt for what he represented. In order to begin the healing process, I let myself feel my self-righteous anger, my disdain, my hatred, my snobbishness. All of it was extremely unpleasant to face.

Another concept I learned from Chuck was that whatever I saw my friend doing to me was really something I must also have been doing to myself. Looking inside of me, I discovered the same conflict. There were inner parts of myself that held opposing beliefs–and I had not even been aware of the conflict. After recognizing this, I could feel fear and remorse being released.

All of this changed my knowledge of myself and my feelings for my friend. As I looked at my friend the next day, he seemed very different. I had no objections at all to who he was or what he said and did. It was easy, because he appeared nothing like the "bad guy" I had previously perceived him to be. By bringing up my buried emotion the night before, I had forgiven myself for being who I thought he was.

Now I could see only his beauty. I could see him as the loving person he truly is. I could see his innocence.

It's true that I had to face some shocking insights and experience some emotional discomfort, but the payoffs for my courage were well worth it. I gained in personal power and self-knowledge. I became an easier person to get along with in a controversial discussion. I became less closed-minded, narrow, judgmental and condescending. My mind loosened. It was easier for me to live with myself. I became more conscious and mature.

It is you who are responsible for what you see, believe, and feel–not the one whom you attack.

Yes, Sweetheart, you resist some feelings. It is what people do. Each has their own preferred defenses. Some become angry when asked to feel. Some fall asleep. Some intellectualize. Some feel cut-off. Some have thoughts that wander....

Do not judge your defenses. Acknowledge them, experience them, and allow them to release into your awareness.

Yet, do not follow them out of your heart. Stay in your heart to feel them, and burn them away. And when they are spent in the furnace of your heart, feel the next thing that asks to be healed.

When you find yourself attacking another in your mind, thinking how they are wrong and you are right, stop your attack and feel the pain it has covered. You will heal yourself as well as the one you offered hate.

It is Heaven's peace that you desire, Sweetheart. To have it, you must be willing to give up attack entirely.

Miracles make minds one in God. They depend on cooperation because the sonship is the sum of all that God created. Miracles therefore reflect the laws of eternity, not of time.

A Course in Miracles, Text, p. 2

CHICKENS

We have a dear friend who lives in California, a therapist named Sabrina. A few years back, we went to the Bay Area to visit her. We rented a vacation house on the ocean and just hung out.

The first evening that we were there, we talked long into the night. Sabrina had recently ended a five-year relationship. I offered to help her finish the grieving process she was in by joining with her, and helping her feel the grief in order to let it go.

She was grateful for the offer, and she did the work with great success. Afterwards, she had professional curiosity about my method. I explained to her, in the best way I knew, what had happened, what I did. I explained that my goal had been to become as close with her as I possibly could, to move my heart and my mind into hers, so that through just the joining itself, a healing would take place.

As we were contemplating this and theorizing about it, we asked ourselves what would happen if we both aimed at each other with the intention of having the deepest, most powerful intimacy possible; not touching each other physically, but moving our minds and hearts towards each other.

So we did it. I started moving into her, and she started moving into me.

An amazing thing began to happen. It started to become exciting! It started to feel almost frightening. It even started to make us dizzy. Our minds began to reel in spirals, but we kept moving toward each other. At a certain point, we had actual contact (again, this was not physical), and that experience of touching was like an explosion. There was blinding light, and the feeling was orgasmic.

It was an experience we could maintain for only a moment before we both fell away from it. It was an entirely overwhelming experience; completely wonderful, incredibly holy, but too much to withstand for more than an instant. We were both just blown away by it.

"Wow...let's do it again!" we said. When we tried to do it again, we could not even come close to repeating the experience. It had been so good, it was just too frightening to repeat.

Over the next few days we tried again, but to no avail. It amazed us to discover how "chicken" we were to experience great love, joy, and intimacy.

> *The power of Sacredness exists independently of time and space, in the holy center of the present moment. To even draw near to it is for Truth to become reality, and to know with no doubt in your soul that Heaven Is Real.*

Miracles are both beginnings and endings, and so they alter the temporal order. They are always affirmations of rebirth, which seem to go back but really go forward. They undo the past in the present, and thus release the future.

A Course in Miracles, Text, p. 2

THE TOKYO COUPLE

Through my seminar work and my counseling practice I have come to the conclusion that most people do not really know how to grieve. It is strange to think that the ability to grieve must be taught or modeled.

While I directed the Support Center, I visited a support group for parents who had lost a child to cancer. The person who headed up the group was a woman whose daughter had died eight years earlier.

She explained that she still could not function in her life very well much of the time, because something would always trigger her grief, and she would just completely fall apart. She was angry that people in her life could not understand why she was not able to deal with her daughter's death yet.

A number of people in the group were in similar shape. None of them envisioned an end to their disabling grief. They saw it as something that would prevent their happiness for the rest of their lives.

A number of times in recent years I have been invited into the hearts of people who have lost their child to death. The experiences of empathically joining with them for healing have been as profoundly vivid and confrontational as my conscious mind could tolerate, yet they have been equally precious and inspiring.

Even the very worst emotional experiences can be dealt with and processed if you know how, or have the right kind of support. I learned a lot about this in Tokyo in 1988. A man whose seven-year-old son was dying of cancer attended one of Chuck's seminars there.

Halfway through it, he was called away to the hospital. The boy died that night with his mother and father in attendance. The father went back to the seminar briefly the next day to thank Chuck and the participants for their support.

About two months later, when we were back in town, the man and his wife attended our lecture, holding hands the whole time. During the 20-minute stretch break, when people were getting up and walking toward the various exits, we stood and went to each other, as if drawn by a magnet. We had no common language, and we did not have an interpreter, but no words were needed.

As we sat down together in the middle of the lecture hall, they looked at me and opened themselves up to me. They completely surrendered their hearts. I let go and let my consciousness fall into theirs.

The three of us tumbled in an emotional free-fall, into the realm of their boy's death, all the time holding tightly to each other's hands. We continued to fall...and fall...and fall through the pain, offering no resistance to it. I almost passed out, it was *that* excruciating.

Then...the end of the tunnel...and soon we were out! Out into the brilliance of life, and relief and love. We looked at each other and laughed and embraced, and cried for joy. The grief they had been feeling was finished, and only minutes had passed. Grief about other aspects of their loss, other issues around the boy's death, would arise later at other times, but they would know that these feelings also could be felt and released.

They were on a potent spiritual journey together, one that would purify, strengthen and evolve them. No path of learning could be more challenging, but they would grow in intimacy and maturity together, and discover the doorway to Heaven on Earth.

No pain is too powerful to feel if, in the same moment, you are sustained by the presence of love. Love is the greater reality, and it exerts its dominion wherever it is given invitation.

If you accept what comes, Sweetheart, and digest it all, it does not really matter what happens in life. You can live in the present, completing the feelings that you create, so that each moment is new, and your future is not merely a repetition of past pain.

HEARTBREAK

By the time most of us reach adulthood, we are full of broken hearts. Some of these broken hearts are easy to remember. Others have partially or completely slipped into the recesses of the subconscious mind. There, forgotten trauma, pain and loss lie hidden, seemingly unimportant. In truth these heartbreaks are constantly affecting us. They determine how we see the world. They make decisions for us. They control our relationships. They keep us contracted and unhappy, and they keep us stuck in repetitive patterns.

There is no good reason to entomb these heartbreaks inside us. If we experience our emotions fully at the times we create them, the feelings move through us without causing any damage. We emerge from this process stronger and wiser. This is how, and perhaps why, we were made.

I witnessed one of my son Christopher's first heartbreaks around the time he turned three years old. He had developed a love for one of my friends, and he courted her with great devotion. When she visited, he would take her by the hand and romantically lead her into his bedroom to play. She was the apple of his eye, his sunshine, his Girlfriend.

One evening our family went to this friend's home for a dinner party. Children were running about the house excitedly when she decided to get everyone seated for dinner. As my son trotted past her with a prized toy in his hand she stopped him, removed the toy from his grasp and ordered him to sit down at the children's table. She was stressed by the pressure of cooking a dinner and pulling off a successful party, and her attention was focused on her situation, not on Christopher.

From across the room I could see my son's face as it shattered. His Beloved had treated him just like any other kid! He would never have treated her so indifferently, without consideration for her feelings. The realization dawned in his mind: she was not in love with him. She did not feel for him what he felt for her.

This understanding hit him with such a wallop of shock and pain that he screamed, and then looked wildly about for me. He ran to me in horror, the emotion too strong for him to talk. My heart went to him, and I felt a pain so sharp and clear it felt as if his heart had been opened with a butcher's cleaver. He clung to me in breathless agony as I carried him to another room.

Small as the incident was, I could feel its devastating effect. All I could do was hold him, feel with him, and say, "I know, I know." Within a couple of minutes enough of the pain had burned away for him to be able to speak.

"Mommy, she made a mistake!" he gasped. "She needs a Time Out!" As he pictured her sitting in her room by herself, sentenced to a Time Out, he said with some satisfaction, "Then she would cry." Within moments he brightened, purity and openness returning to his face. "But *I* would save her!" he exclaimed as he jumped from my lap to run and join the others. The heartbreak was over.

I was floored by the beauty of the process I had witnessed. By simply allowing the natural completion of an emotional experience, my son was not only saved from a broken heart, he had benefited from the experience of forgiving a friend when she made a mistake. He actually had a better self-image after the experience, and he had tasted the love that lies at the end of every heartbreak.

*When you have learned to recognize and honor
your own emotional self, to do only what you truly
want to do, you will be, for the first time, truly safe
and harmless towards those around you....*

MATURITY

To be able to feel emotion without feeling self-centered or self-pity, and without the need to act on the feelings, or take them out on those around us, is a sign of emotional development and maturity.

As adults, we focus on developing our intellectual self and perhaps our spiritual self, but seldom our emotional self, because we have been under the impression that we were not supposed to feel. Expressing our feelings by attacking others only got us into trouble.

Learning to control our behavior when experiencing emotion was an important step in our development, but we paid a heavy price. We learned to stuff down our emotions so that we would not feel them and so it would not be difficult to control our behavior. Stuffing emotion, however, leads to dissociation and emotional, mental and physical health problems.

In one seminar, a Chinese woman asked about the origin of her severe and chronic back pain. She professed an inability to feel emotion, which she thought stemmed from her upbringing: her parents taught her not to speak or move in their presence.

On closer examination, she recalled a fight she had with her mother when she was eleven years old. The confrontation climaxed with the mother tearing off the child's clothing, beating her, and throwing her out of the house. She hid in the neighborhood, naked, for hours.

The person I held as she wailed was not truly the 30-year-old woman in my seminar, but the battered and shamed child who felt her world had come to an end.

At last she was able to let her emotional blockade fall apart. She rebuilt herself in the presence of love, allowing it to comfort and mother her, and support the broken child to blossom into emotional maturity.

Our challenge as emotional beings is to learn to control our behavior and experience our feelings at the same time. This is maturity.

As children, perhaps, we could not do it. As mature adults, we can trust ourselves to feel everything and still not indulge in those feelings or hurt anyone around us.

Once this ability to feel is recovered, we can then learn to be kind to ourselves by not sacrificing. It is important to recognize that sacrificing to others in order to be kind to their emotional selves, while denying the needs and feelings of our own emotional selves, is still an unkindness.

We have taught ourselves to be enormously, continuously, unkind to ourselves, thinking that we have learned to be mature. This kind of behavior—being "tough" on ourselves, or self-denying—is not maturity; it merely shows lack of awareness and responsibility.

The sacrifice and self-denial that is so often seen as admirable, actually engenders guilt and resentment in those who receive it. Since we are all one, what is true for one will be true for all.

*Every time someone enters your mind, Sweet-
heart, every time you are with another, you could be
giving them the gift of your open heart. Each time
you think of them with your heart open and extending, even if it is only for a few moments, they will
prosper. They will blossom. They will be lifted up.
They will feel loved, and they will know they have
value.*

*You can nurture the people you love and care
for, and even the people you fear (who need help),
by attending to them as you would tend to a
garden...simply by holding them in your heart.*

BEDTIME

One of my greatest pleasures is sharing love with my
children. It is beautiful to see them grow up knowing about
love; playing with it, asking for it, giving it to others. Maybe
the best thing is watching them give it to each other.

A few years ago, during one of our nightly bedtime love
exchanges, I asked my children what love felt like to them.
My three-year-old daughter laughed her angelic baby laugh
and declared that it felt like, "Beautiful Barbies, and ponies,
rainbows, and hearts!"

My five-year-old son just said, "Love feels like love. But
Mommy's love feels like Mommy love, and Daddy's love
feels like Daddy love."

I have often seen the children respond to a person in
distress, whether it is physical or emotional, by putting their
hands on them and loving them (diagnosing that the person
needed some love). I have watched them lavish love and
affection on relatives they've never met, or have not seen for
a long time, or on new acquaintances that take their fancy.
And when they have what they call a "bad feeling," they

know how to experience it, asking for adult support and help to feel it through to the finish.

It is a wonder to me to see them be so emotionally sophisticated. Even when they were very little they could express their feelings in such terms as, "It feels like I'm afraid of a dragon inside," or "It feels like monsters."

I probably make at least as many errors in parenting each day as I enjoy successes. Fortunately, I have the comfort of knowing that when I make mistakes (if we have a fight, if I become irritable or mean), we can unravel the damage, and grow together in the process.

I remember blowing up at the kids one night when they were ages three and five. Chuck was out of town, and I'd had a long day of caring for the kids, keeping house, running our business, and trying to write this book. When my anger was finished and remorse had set in, I apologized for my behavior and asked their forgiveness. They both simply smiled and embraced me. Christopher explained, "It doesn't matter if you get mad at us, Mommy, because we know you love us!"

I'm embarrassed at times to see my children handle an emotional situation in a kinder and more mature way than I. Yet I have confidence that whatever happens in our relationship, there is no damage that would be so great we could not repair it through forgiveness, love, and intimacy.

Miracles honor you because you are lovable. They dispel illusions about yourself and perceive the light in you. They thus atone for your errors by freeing you from your nightmares. By releasing your mind from the imprisonment of your illusions, they restore your sanity.

A Course in Miracles, Text, p. 3

ALL YOU NEED IS LOVE

A couple of years ago a friend confided to me that she was at her wit's end with her son. He was a hyperactive ten-year-old with problems at school, which were exacerbated by his father's deployment to the Middle East (via the U.S. Marine Corps and Operation Desert Storm). In the weeks since his father's departure, his behavior had deteriorated to such a degree that his teachers were almost to the point of desperation. His mother, with all of the financial and emotional pressures she was under, seriously felt she was at the end of her rope.

Teachers' and counselors' recommendations for behavior modification using natural consequences did nothing to abate the problem. Medication changes and dietary restrictions were no help.

I suggested that she try something that had always worked for me when my children's behavior bothered me. I suggested she treat the child's need instead of the symptoms, by providing the boy with more love and physical contact.

With my own children I have always seen a direct correlation between our level of connectedness and their behavior. When their basic need for the sustenance of parental love and contact is satisfied, they're happier people, and easier to be with. I suggested that she begin that evening, a Friday, by sitting with him and holding him while they watched television, and touching him or holding his hand when they went out together. She could concentrate on nursing his heart with hers. Loving him, nurturing him, mothering him.

She followed my directions, and was amazed at the immediate results. They had the happiest weekend together, just hanging out. By Sunday when a friend needed her help and attention, the boy was willing to entertain himself outside for an hour and a half without interrupting. Generally he would have been in the house interrupting his mother at least every ten minutes.

The biggest surprise was a telephone call she received from her son's teacher on Monday afternoon. The teacher excitedly asked if she had changed the boy's medication. My friend said no. The teacher asked if she had been doing something else differently. My friend asked why. With amazement, the teacher said that all that school day the boy had been calm and happy, showing no behavior problems whatsoever. The teacher's parting remark was, "Whatever you're doing, keep it up!"

At the bottom of any unkind, unhappy, or malicious act, there is a call for love. It takes great wisdom to remember this as you face attack, but love is the greatest healer.

> Miracles are natural. When they do
> not occur, something has gone wrong.
> *A Course in Miracles*, Text, p. 1

THE GREATEST REALITY

Ten years ago I was blessed with my first experience of looking into eyes so unobstructed that I could see all the way to God. They were the eyes of my infant godson, Cooper.

I assisted Cooper's mother (my dear friend, Peggy) at his birth. After he was out, free, received into the arms of his joyful parents, I was allowed to hold him.

Tiny but alert, he looked at, into, and through me. As I looked back I was astounded; it was as if there was no one inside him.

I could see into forever, where the light of distant stars twinkled and sang to me. He was both completely empty and fathomlessly deep. Nothing of the past showed in his gaze, no personality weaved of pain.

Only the breathtaking Omnipresent was there, abiding. He showed me what it is like for a human being to look at life as it is in the present moment, rather than to look out at the world seeing the pain of the past projected there.

When I enter intimacy with people, when Heaven's love is working its way through our hearts, their eyes show me their present experience. Usually their present experience is their past; past emotion that was left unfelt, or dissociation from old feelings of disappointment, grief and trauma.

If I want, I can even read the story line, feeling and sensing the events that silently pour out of their eyes to be known and shared. In intimacy's safety, defenses can be laid aside, and they can risk to be aligned with their heart in the present moment. It is only in the present moment, the Eternal Now, that the past can be released, and healing can occur.

120

And when the love has done its work, when they are experiencing the grace of love's comfort, they can truly look out of their eyes and see a world in which Love is the greatest Reality.

Our attention is like the cursor of a computer; wherever it is moved on our screen of attention, we have the power to act and create. Usually our attention is placed on ourselves–our needs and desires, our hurts, our problems and conflicts, our addictions, our comforts... but as long as our attention is placed on ourselves, we are caught in separation and self-consciousness, and Beauty cannot reveal itself. The most important thing to learn in life is control over where we place our cursor of attention.

If you place your attention on any one person well enough, Sweetheart, they will reveal themselves, and become your bridge to a greater reality of Love and Joy.

Miracles should inspire gratitude, not awe. You should thank God for what you really are. The children of God are holy and the miracle honors their holiness, which can be hidden but never lost.

A Course in Miracles, Text, p. 3

GOD'S EYES

A profound revelation came in the French Pyrenees Mountains a few years ago, where Chuck and I were conducting a seminar that summer. It was lovely spot. The slopes were covered with wild flowers and butterflies. Our children were delighted with the goats that tripped past our lodge.

A certain young man who was attending the workshop caught my attention from the start. He was noteworthy to me because he seemed extremely self-conscious and repressed. I thought of him as the classic "cold fish"...very much an intellectual, and greatly in resistance to the workshop.

Once during tea-break this fellow stood ahead of me in line to fill his tea cup with hot water. When his cup was full, he turned around. Discovering that I had been standing behind him, he was so startled that he jumped and spilled the hot water all over himself.

Symbolically, this was a very clear message about his emotional state (water being a subconscious symbol for emotion), and perhaps of his fear that I would bring his emotions to the surface. From that point on I took an especially strong interest in him. I felt as though he had given me a special signal through that communication.

Later that day, during the seminar, this man spoke up for the first time. He expressed that he wanted, above all things, to be able to have a direct experience of God; to know that God was real. Deep within me, I could feel that this was what he wanted from me, and somehow, that I could respond to that need.

As my husband took the rest of the workshop in another direction, I sat beside this man and began to look into him, to try to find him. I could not feel him inside his body. I could not see him inside of his eyes. There was only distance, deadness, and dissociation. I groped through the nothingness, determined that I would reach him. Although I knew some progress was being made, I had no idea how much, or how vast the cavern was in which I was swimming.

Finally, some time later, I realized that I could not find this man in the place he was hiding because I had not yet healed that place inside myself. I also had no feeling of God. Like him, I also felt distant from God's presence. And I recognized that if I was to give this man the gift he most wanted, I would first have to give it to myself.

Turning my awareness self-ward, I burned into my own soul to find the place that anguished in its loneliness, in its separation. And as I felt it, I began to feel this young man as my friend. He had become my learning partner, my healing partner. He was my equal. We were the same.

Then, as I pulled at the skein of his inner world, I could finally feel some substance and experience some interaction. Intuitively, I knew that if I looked into his eyes hard enough, long enough, and with enough expectancy, that I would be able to see God there. I would be able to see what we were both looking for.

At long last, in a heartbreak of purity and grace, I could feel this man awaken and begin to look out of his eyes. His eyes took on a look of wonder and great surprise at being awakened. Then I saw a look of appreciation and thankfulness so deep, and so beautiful, that it changed my life.

As I continued to look into his eyes, yet another dramatic change came over them. There, looking out of his eyes, was God! Somehow it was the same look that I had seen in the pink and golden clouds of the great ray of Love I had seen years before. It was a look of humor, vast intelligence, and love.

To see that love shining out at me, flowing into me, satisfied the deepest hunger. My consciousness was lifted. And this man, his face now beautiful, laughing and celebrating, his heart bursting with joy, embraced me. As I looked around the room, others from the workshop were watching, beginning to share in the experience of what was taking place.

As I looked in the eyes around me, I found that if I looked even a little bit, I could see God there too. God was looking at me from every set of eyes that I looked into! I was lifted higher in my transcendence, and as I looked around the room, I could see that even the walls of the room were looking back at me with God's love! It was a powerful confrontation. The experience washed my heart and mind as tears fell from my eyes.

One woman came up to me, her face beaming. She had an obvious desire to give me the gift of her love as well. I looked into her eyes, to see God there.

She looked back at me with great expectation. I looked for God, and I looked for God, but I could not see God. And I thought, "Oh no! Poor thing, don't let on that you can't see love in her eyes."

I did not know what was wrong. So I looked back into someone else's eyes. I could see God there, shining, smiling, laughing out at me. The experience filled me, until again I began to cry from the confrontation of love.

The next morning, when we began the workshop, Chuck worked with the group first. He and I were both at the front of the room, and as he took the workshop in a certain direction, I found myself looking at the person seated right in front of me. Who should it be but that woman again! And still, she had that expectant smile on her face.

I could see she believed she was offering me something extraordinary. I just could not feel it, could not see it. I also realized that she would not be sitting in front of me, and I would not have this opportunity of time and space to deal with it, if it was not all happening for a purpose. So I settled in to explore what I could experience in this woman's face, and heart, and eyes.

As I looked at her I began to realize something. I realized that her eyes looked just like my mother's. Then, as I looked into her eyes, I could begin to feel the feeling that I always felt when I was in my mother's presence. I began to have the complete experience of being with my mother. I could smell the way my mother smells to me. I could sense her presence. The experience was not a comfortable one. Actually, it was extremely uncomfortable.

I used my courage to move even closer into the experience of being with my mother. Seeing her looking out through this woman's eyes, I began to recognize that, in fact, God was looking out at me. God was looking at me through the eyes of my mother!

It was one of those dreadful realizations–I saw God–only to discover that God was my *mother!* I felt so bad all of a sudden; a terrible sense of guilt and fear.

I realized that when I had seen God looking out at me through people's eyes the day before, they were men's eyes. It was very much an experience of seeing God as expressed through my father's eyes.

It seemed that God was able to reach me through my masculine parent, but I still resisted receiving God through my feminine parent. This reflected judgements and projections I had on my mother that I had not yet cleaned up by seeing them as reflections of myself. It showed me the degree of damage that I still carried in my feminine side (every person, male or female, has both a masculine and a feminine aspect to their nature).

I also realized how important and precious our first relationships are. How much we depend on our parents in order to have a balanced experience of God.

Once this had dawned on me I saw the tremendous value of hanging in there through this process with the woman in front of me. I gave myself as best I could to the burn of emotion. I sat for the longest time, excruciating in the pain of having to receive love from my mother; of seeing her as my equal; of seeing her and myself as the same.

For so many years I had subtly withdrawn from my mother's love as a way of taking revenge on her. Revenge for childhood grievances, and for guilt I felt about being a bad daughter. To have to receive her love at last was at one and the same time exquisite pleasure and horrendous pain.

I stayed in that experience until I felt only the pleasure, and could finally receive what this woman's knowing expression had been offering me since the day before–my mother loved me. She had always only loved me. It was a big lesson; it was a big seminar for me.

We did not work in France again for another year. When we did return, someone came up to see me after our evening lecture. Looking at the man, I did not recognize him. He did not look familiar in any way. I could feel his heart, and feel that I had a relationship with him. I could tell that I had already joined with him, because an open pathway straight into his heart was available to me.

I asked a bilingual person who he was, and they answered me with great delight that he was the "cold fish" from the seminar the previous year. Yet this man was full of life, full of spirit! He was suave and dashing! He laughed with delight, and gave me a huge bear hug.

Since that time I have witnessed many people come back to life in this way. I have shared the rapture and wonder as they stepped out of the grave they had made for themselves behind their eyes, and I have laughed with them as the mirth of God poured out to the world.

If you place yourself at the level of equality with others, anyone can be your teacher. Allow yourself to be taught by everyone!

Recognize the truth and wisdom in what they say. They have their intelligence, too. Differences are only temporary.

How willing are you to be equal with others, Sweetheart? You must see them this way in order to progress. It is how you shine your light into the darkness...willingness to be equal instead of special.

Whenever you are in conflict with others, it is because you are not willing to see them as your equals. Practice looking upon even those with whom you are in the most resistance with equality.

The miracle acknowledges everyone as your brother and mine. It is a way of perceiving the universal mark of God.

A Course in Miracles, Text, p. 4

THREE-PIECE SUIT

Early in 1990 I was invited to teach a seminar for a training company in Taipei. Generally, when I lead seminars, I teach from the psycho-therapeutic model that Chuck and I have developed over the years, the Psychology of Vision, using my own techniques and style, and focusing on a theme of my own choice.

In this case, however, the seminar company wanted me to teach our Psychology of Vision theories within the framework of a more conventional, traditional format, such as goal setting, time management, etc. The company asked for this particular structure because they thought it would be a format that the seminar participants (primarily Taiwanese businessmen) could relate to and understand.

Although I felt confident I could deliver a good conventional-style seminar, I felt a little outside my comfort zone. My personal style of work is so radically feminine, so deeply intimate and emotional, I felt somewhat self-conscious. The picture of a room full of Chinese business men and women–in my mind the quintessential inscrutable masters of the bottom-line, the epitome of the masculine mind in action–well, it did not fill me with a sense of ease. Would they want or value what I wanted to give them?

Regardless, I packed up the kids and headed off on a twelve-hour overnight flight to Taipei. We were excited to see what Taiwan would be like.

The people were delightful, the food was delicious, and my kids loved their baby sitter (whom the Taiwanese sweetly misnomered a "baby sister"). My only real difficulty was that the children stayed on Hawaiian time; they slept while I worked, and wanted to play when I wanted to sleep.

The seminar began on a Friday evening, the second night we were there. Sure enough, the room filled with business men and women, still wearing the suits they had worn to work that day. They looked like a tough crowd. One man, a polished looking fellow in a three-piece suit, looked especially inscrutable and unreachable.

The seminar moved along at a good clip. As the weekend progressed, the information and theories were well received, and the seminar company owners were quite pleased with how the seminar was going. So much so, in fact, that I felt able to ask a bold question. I asked if I could have the next morning, the morning of the last day of the seminar, to do what I wanted to do with the group. Without hesitation, the owners said, "Yes!"

When the morning session began, I explained to the group that I would start to do some work within the group mind. I dismissed my interpreter (because words would not be needed), and put on some music. I then reached through my heart and pulled everyone in the room into rapport, into intimacy.

I moved through the group, stopping here and there to pull the sundry mavericks and resisters into contact with the love. Soon, most all of the people were crying or sobbing; some cried out as old pain left them.

Unlike any other group I had ever worked with, this bunch was highly mobile. They all had their own chairs, yet coming from a culture accustomed to sitting on the floor, they would often sit on the carpet. Wherever I sat down to work with one person, the others would scurry over and sit around us, kindergarten style, intently watching everything that took place.

Sometimes one of them would bring me a friend or spouse who was too self-denying to reach out for help themselves. The intensity of the love in the room grew to the point that the miracles were coming quickly and easily. I began to feel that the gateway to Heaven was open.

As the love was able to break into the heart of a defiant young woman who was clinging to me, I felt myself touched from behind. I turned to see who wanted me, and was warmed to see that it was my Three-Piece Suit.

He sat crouched, close to the floor, his eyes averted in humility. Only his arm was extended, his hand still touching me to help him feel the love. Bless his heart, I thought, as I reached for him.

He began to sob, and then to cry as his heart opened and the love washed through him. I could feel God loving him through me.

As a group we stayed in the love for four hours, finally breaking for our meal. Needless to say, the seminar wrapped up on an inspired note. The participants all seemed to have gone through life-changing transformations.

When the seminar ended, they were so excited and drunk with happiness that they stayed in the room for hours, hugging, laughing, and playing (generally, hugging does not often occur in the Chinese culture, so they got a real kick out of it).

I remember them taking turns running the length of the seminar room into each other's arms, and also building human pyramids several stories high that collapsed into mounds of hilarity. I had to remind myself that only two days before their business-like appearance had intimidated me!

Of all the expressions of appreciation and love that evening, the one that filled me with the most joy came from my Three-Piece Suit. With tears streaming down his cheeks, his eyes alive with a new radiance, he told me he had received the most valuable of gifts: For the first time, he could actually feel his own love for his wife and his children. It meant the world to him.

No one is so independent or separate that they do not need their hearts, do not need to feel and express love, do not ache to return to the safekeeping of being known and cared for by Heaven. It is all waiting for you, Sweetheart, available through connection with another human heart.

Miracles praise God through you.
They praise Him by honoring His
creations, affirming their perfection.
They heal because they deny body-
identification and affirm spirit-iden-
tification.

A Course in Miracles, Text, p. 3

IRRESISTIBILITY

In the summer of 1990, Chuck and I conducted a five-day
workshop in the Swiss Alps, entitled "Death and Transformation." There were a hundred people participating, many
of them doctors and nurses. And they were not just any
people, they were Swiss.

Swiss are known for their prudence and control, and this
group was no exception. They strived to keep control of their
emotional state as best they could, fearing the unknown
experience of "letting go." Chuck and I plied them with
information, swaddled them in love and let them cook.

On the morning of the second day, they blew. The
pressure cooker of the workshop had cooked them to the
point that their reserve could not prevent the birth. I had
internally dealt with the resistance, burned it away, digested
the fear, and reached the center of the group mind. When that
point was reached, some people began to scream as their old
pain came to the surface. Many cried. Most everyone felt
some form of emotion.

From that point on the workshop was more exciting and
juicy. People could reach down inside themselves and
discover parts of them they had not known existed. They
recovered memories, emotions and sentiments that they had
packed away long before. But there was one fellow I could
not reach; he was a self-proclaimed "sad-sack" whom I'll call

Emil. He was ever the pessimist, always depressed, certain that life could not ever make it up to him for the disappointments he'd suffered in his childhood.

At one point, I virtually stopped the workshop to reach for him, to pull on him, to bring him into contact. Yet he could not, he would not. He was too invested in being right about life. He took too much pleasure from his pain.

I surrendered, letting him be as he was, but still keeping faith that the love that had poured out to him would wait for his welcome. I knew that at some point it would render him defenseless.

The workshop continued with its peaks and valleys, its moments of comedy and tenderness. Every person present moved more into communion.

Finally, the biggest resistance of the workshop was unearthed. We reached a place in the group mind where people had, in the past, given up and experienced an emotional death.

These lifeless parts were well protected and defended. Between my conscious awareness and these metaphorically dead places there was a sea of loss, anger, loneliness, and inertia. To the eye, I may not have appeared active, but in my inner reality I was churning, chopping, digesting and burning. I consumed my way toward their lifelessness.

At one point, the person whose awareness was most available, most near the surface, began to awaken. Her defense disintegrated. She became reachable, and she began to feel loved. The group mind broke through into a level of consciousness in which it was possible for the love to begin to clear out their hearts and be received. As the group mind converted, many began to cry, and their hearts began to loosen.

The people began to experience the focusing clarity of being truly awake. As more and more of the participants tumbled into their feelings, a shift occurred, and we began to see the light at the end of the tunnel. We began to be able to feel love filling our hearts; love that descended to us from a Divine Source. Hearts filled to overflowing.

It began with one, then two, three, four...more and more faces opening up with amazement. They were feeling loved. They were feeling delight. They were feeling bliss. And these prudent, controlled, sensible people were on their feet, dancing, hugging the people next to them, hardly knowing what to do with themselves.

Heaven was so present and had created such a stronghold that I knew there was nothing that would not be granted. There was nothing we could not have. There was no one who could resist the love—it was too compelling.

I looked up from the person who had been birthing. Yes, from across the room Emil was looking back at me. Just one good tug on his heart...and he smiled, then laughed, because he knew the jig was up. He knew he could no longer keep love away.

He and I stood as one, and walked to the center of the room, arms extended to each other, weeping for joy, filled with gratitude, sensing the angels' thankfulness. Everyone felt our rapture.

The Heavens opened many times during that workshop, each time bringing nearly unbearable tenderness, happiness, and intimacy. These outpourings of grace are the most awesome of times for me. They are the times I feel most humble, and the times I feel the most grandeur.

The next summer we returned to Switzerland for a 10-day seminar entitled, "The Miracle of Love." True to its name, the seminar was extraordinary from start to finish. A deep and full presence of love was in attendance from the first moment we stood in front of the group. During my sessions, most of the participants were able to sit peacefully in the flow of love and bliss as their buried issues and emotions were loosened and lifted up and out.

I found that many could go through the process of opening up an old pain and releasing it up into love within a few minutes, or even just moments. Even those who wrestled with the process and released the emotion more dramatically were easily pulled through. The whole seminar was a miracle.

Emil was there and did excellent work, experiencing many breakthroughs in his relationship with his father, mother, and the rest of the world. Every day he became more happy, more social, even suave and debonair.

At the end of the seminar he stood to thank us all for our contributions to him, describing with awe in his voice the man he had become. He could not only feel his own love for every person there, he had become a man who could thoroughly experience the distinctly recognizable love of each individual. He had the look of a man who had awakened to find himself in Heaven.

> *Heaven is real! It is your rightful reality. All that is needed is for you to value it, to sense your way towards it, and to receive it as your own.*
>
> *To live in Heaven you must have willingness to be wrong about many things—wrong about who you are, how much you are loved, and the purpose of your life. Surrender, Sweetheart. The jig is up!*

It is through your feminine aspect that you receive, Sweetheart. It is the same for men as it is for women. The feminine is the vehicle for grace, for healing, for relationship and for love. Without it life is incomplete, hollow, empty.

Every soul needs its feminine half, because it is this which will lead you back to Heaven, and teach you how to receive God's nurturing and care....

BLACK AND WHITE

I grew up in a time in which the feminine was devalued. Even the term effeminate was an insult. Recent years have been interesting times in this regard. Cultures that for thousands of years have highly valued most things masculine, and distrusted and disparaged most things feminine, are experiencing upheaval as the pendulum begins to swing back into balance.

In recent years our society has begun to revalue the feminine. At a psychological and spiritual level this offers us great opportunity for development, expression and satisfaction. Men and women both are recognizing that without the development and expression of their feminine nature they are incomplete and imbalanced.

Interestingly enough, the feminine was perhaps the first aspect of God to be recognized by humanity. For the greater part of human history, God was worshipped as a female. It is only in the past few thousand years that the majority of cultures have conceived God to be masculine.

Some cultures still worship a feminine God, or worship both masculine and feminine Gods. The Hindu religion recognizes the feminine aspect of God, and worships Her in the form of the Great Mother, as well as other feminine deities.

The feminist movement, which began as a social movement and evolved into a political movement, has now further evolved (at least in some of its branches) into a spiritual movement in which women are rediscovering and relating to the feminine aspect of God, "The Goddess." I once saw a bumper sticker that I thought was provocative and cute. It read, "God Is Coming Soon (And Is She Pissed!)."

The modern masculine religions probably developed, in part, as a reaction against the powerful feminine religions that preceded them. In the same way, you do not hear the Goddess worshipers honoring the masculine aspect of God. Would not a Creator logically contain both aspects if we were truly created in His/Her image?

I understand that Martin Luther believed in the feminine aspect of God, but left Her out of the blueprint for Protestantism because he became convinced that Muslims would never convert to a religion that had a female deity. Surely a religion that teaches of a Father and a Son must consider that a Mother is a necessary part of the equation.

I always love it when, in the course of leading a workshop, a major healing breakthrough occurs for me. One such opportunity was a workshop that I taught for women in 1989, entitled "Awakening the Goddess Within." Many women in our Western culture were greatly interested in this subject at the time. That same weekend, on the other side of the globe, student radicals in Tianamen Square were erecting their Goddess of Liberty.

One of the goals that I had for the training was to assist the women in becoming acquainted with, and comfortable with, the less accepted side of their nature...the qualities that our culture frowns on, but that are integral and necessary components of the feminine mind. Qualities recognized as classically feminine include: birth, death, sexuality, passion, nurturing, destruction, darkness, and the ability to receive and absorb.

We have been taught to disavow our aggression and our passion and sexuality. I hoped with all my heart that the workshop would give us the freedom to once again, or perhaps only for the first time, experience these aspects of ourselves. Strange as it sounds, aggression is an indispensable ingredient in developing the capacity to relate and have intimacy, and all of these "darker qualities" are necessary aspects of our humanness.

The workshop started off with a tremendous connectedness, even though most of the women expressed discomfort at being in the company of a roomful of other women. Many said they usually did their best to avoid such experiences. Not trusting women, not feeling safe, not liking women, they did not enjoy their company. Still, they felt inexorably drawn to this seminar. There was also a fairly large contingent of lesbians who often found themselves in the company of other women, but seldom straight women.

It was an easy group to get into, an easy group to feel. Soon, we were enveloped within a common consciousness, and we took a ride deep, deep, into our minds; deep into the Feminine. The women began to "pop." Emotions came up and out freely. Compassion poured from our hearts–we healed and forgave and loved. And then, on the morning of the second day, an especially advanced and talented participant took us all on an interesting adventure into the Feminine Mind.

She began to describe a feeling of blackness, darkness, like a cave inside herself. She felt afraid to go in by herself, but willingly took all of us with her into the cavern. As we progressed, she felt the floor of the cave give way, and she fell, landing, to her disgust, in a pile of bones and ashes. I sensed that something miraculous waited for us, and I asked her if we had discovered the cremation ground.

The woman had studied religious and spiritual practices enough to know what I was suggesting. She let us know that she was in the territory of the mind that was the domain of the Dark Goddess. As she embraced the experience of the pure and utter emptiness of the cremation ground, she began to be indwelt by the Great Mother Herself.

A surge of adrenaline and a sense of mystery filled me, leaving me with goose bumps from head to toe. It was almost too frightening, too beautiful, too powerful a sensation. Regardless, I seized the opportunity.

I turned down the lights, put on eerie but beautiful "underworld" music, and told the group that we were beginning a ritual. It would be a ritual of our own creation, entirely personal, entirely individual.

I would provide the safety in this time and place. They could do anything they wanted to do, felt moved to do. *Anything* that came to their mind, except to hurt themselves or another individual. In the half hour that followed, the 75 women let go of their culturally defined barriers, and experienced the wildness and beauty of their fury. They *became* their passion, aggression, and strength.

Some leaped and pounded. Some chanted and danced. Some twirled, some screamed, some yelled, some laughed.

It was the most beautiful sight to me; the most ecstatic and exciting feeling. I sat at the front of the room, containing everyone there within my awareness, experiencing it all within me. And with tears of profound humility and thankfulness, I offered this ritual, this worship, up to Heaven as a gift, my gift to the Goddess. Perhaps She had not been celebrated in this way for thousands of years.

In my mind's eye, just as I lifted the gift up to offer it to Her, I was caught. I was snagged by fear. An old, half-forgotten but still potent belief captured me. I was offering this experience to the Goddess, the same goddess who had Dionysus as her consort. The same Dionysus which was made into the devil by later Judeo-Christian philosophy.

What if I was misguided? What if this act of feminine resurrection was in fact nothing more than a devil worship? What if I was wrong, and an evil power had tricked me into guiding these innocents into corruption?

I was suspended, caught in the dilemma. The situation had forced my hand, forced the conflict, the cognitive dissonance into my mind. I had to discern the truth! All I could think to do was to *feel* into the question. I trusted somehow that I could feel the truth, that I could feel the answer. And as I did, I could see only healing and liberation and loving integrity in the ritual expression before me.

The answer was resounding: what these women were doing was true. It was honest, it was real, it was empowering. It was a corner of the human mind allowed life and expression that had previously been judged and denied.

This recognition broke through a membrane that had bound me for a long, long time. I finished offering the gift to Heaven. And as I released it, something powerful took place within me. My mind stopped. Something broke. I felt a disintegration take place.

I could feel the belief in right and wrong, in good and evil, in white and black, in masculine and feminine, shatter and scramble. The pieces shivered and vibrated into each other. An integration and healing took place at a deep level of my mind. Good and evil no longer existed as separate forces. Now I experienced unity and wholeness, where before there had been duality and separation.

The women loved the exercise. Many had a direct experience of the Goddess indwelling them. Many retrieved their sense of power and passion. I believe everyone gained a new sense of self acceptance and freedom. The most dramatic result I saw emerge from the workshop was the transformation of a group of women who did not like each other into a group of feminists (by my definition of the word): women who love women.

Prayer is the medium of miracles. It is a means of communication of the created with the Creator. Through prayer love is received, and through miracles love is expressed.

A Course in Miracles, Text, p. 1

RECEIVING

Recently Chuck and I had the honor of serving as witnesses at the civil wedding ceremony of two very dear friends, Alma & Rony; two souls who are so loving, kind and bright, they are quite obviously "angels without wings."* They would later go on to orchestrate one of the greatest weddings of all time in the south of France, but it was their small intimate legal ceremony in London that we were able to attend.

Afterwards, we all went to lunch at a charming restaurant with delicious food, taking over a large table in a private atrium. I was seated to the left of the groom, but I did not yet know the other witnesses who sat beside and across from me.

It was a lovely celebration and the grace flowed like the fine wine that poured. The young man who sat to my left was an interesting individual. He was clever and successful, but as we talked it became apparent to me that he had little happiness in his life. He seemed uncomfortable in himself, and dissatisfied. I could sense his need and loneliness, and I decided that, since the flow of grace was so available, I would receive some of it for him.

I casually placed my hand on his back as I chatted with the fascinating couple across from me. Soon he had animat-

*A term I borrow from Alma, who has made it her life's work to find and to film the saints of our time. This is clearly a case of "it takes one to know one."

edly joined the conversation, actually taking it over. He turned the topic of conversation to the needs of men.

A man's life boils down to his incessant search for the Great Nipple on which to suckle, he announced. He pulled the groom into the discussion for confirmation–didn't he agree?

The groom's face registered shock, not so much for the obvious reasons, but because his friend was no great lover of women. It was probably one of the last things he had expected to hear him say.

The conversation moved along other lines, but I continued to direct the grace and love into the young man's heart. After awhile, he stopped talking and simply sat with a somewhat dopey-looking grin on his face.

Then this man, still a boy, really, lowered himself to lie with his head on my lap, a blissful look of cherubic satisfaction on his face. Since I was in the experience of grace with him, it felt perfectly sweet and natural to me.

In a while the first course was served. The young man sat up, and my attention focused more on the group as a whole. The holiness of Alma and Rony's relationship was such a blessing to the planet. What an honor and joy it was to be with them!

It was not until the next evening that we were able to spend some time hanging out with them and another London buddy, Michael. As we relived the pleasure of the previous day, Alma and Rony were in stitches recalling the incongruence of the sight of their friend's head in my lap at the wedding luncheon. It was just so totally out of character for him! On top of that, Rony had seen the fellow this morning. He was still so happy, it was as if he were walking on air.

I believe what that young man said at the restaurant was true. I believe that the feminine aspect of us, especially as it is embodied in a woman, is designed to receive the nectar of loving Heavenly grace. When the feminine has received it to

142

overflowing, the sweetness can be shared in a stream of energy that, at the subtle level, could be likened to providing Mother's milk. It is a nurturing that satisfies the inner child's need for Mothering.

In this way, I see a mother as the center of the family, the source of nurturing comfort and care for husband and children. No one is more popular than "Mamma" when she can supply this basic human need.

Women I have known through seminars instinctively recognized this ability to "receive for" others. Frequently they had offered the gift of this healing nectar in their earliest relationships, only to shut it down out of fear of being "eaten alive." Their gratitude at being able to open this channel again has been great.

It is deeply satisfying to a woman to be able to bring this delicious honeyed energy into human expression. To me it seems a most important aspect of love-making. The feminine aspect brings in pleasure so exciting and enticing that the couple is lifted into rapture.

Not to limit the experience of "bringing in grace" to women. Chuck, who is exquisitely masculine, is a self-proclaimed "hand-maiden to the Mother." Many of the most accomplished students of my methods are men from all around the world, who are quite secure in their masculinity.

They are able to link their hearts and minds with the same rapture that I know, and give it as a gift to the people they reach out to. It is wonderful to have them as staff in our seminars; more hearts and eyes and hands for Heaven to work through; angels without wings in service to the Mother.

It is your heart's desire to grow in grace and love. Allow the gifts of life to nourish and fill you, and flow out to the world for the benefit of all.

When you have realized God's love, you will no longer see anyone as different from yourself. Nationality, race, culture, social class, sex, sexual preference, age, intellectual level, physical appearance...all fall away in importance.

Such qualities are only the thinnest veneer covering the unfathomable depth of our Oneness. God sits in the heart of each human being; we are all the same.

Extend the boundaries of your love to include all people–all living sentient creatures–so that you may awaken others to the one Reality which sustains and unites us all.

TEARING DOWN THE WALLS

At one weekend seminar in the Pacific West Coast, a number of First Nation people (Native Americans) were in attendance. One group of 30 had driven a bus eight hours to make it. It took courage for them to come, and it was not easy for them to be there.

During the Friday evening introduction, I made reference to a unique expression of East Indians (from India); I guess it was on my mind because we had been with Indian friends in London just a couple of days before, and it fit in well with what I was saying. Unfortunately, the First Nation people assumed I was referring to them, calling attention to their presence in the room, and worst of all, using the politically incorrect term "Indian." To top it all off, they were also upset to be called "east" Indians when they were from the west.

On Saturday morning the group from the bus waited outside the seminar room, unwilling to come in. I left the seminar to talk with them, and by the grace of God, after much debate, they decided to go back into the seminar room for five minutes to give me a chance to explain the misunderstanding. One particular young man was especially influential in that decision-making process. After hearing my explanation, they all stood and left again; 20 minutes later, all but three of them returned.

During my section of the seminar that afternoon, the love flowed, and the work was easy. When it came time to look that young man in the eyes, I could feel the love hit him with great impact. A look of profound surprise appeared on his face, and he smiled quizzically at me. It made me very happy.

It was a wonderful workshop, and the Anglos deeply appreciated the presence of the First Nation people–especially since we had almost lost them! One older fellow, a man who joked about the dilemma of being an Indian who was a cowboy by profession, revealed that he had lost his family due to his (now recovering) alcoholism. His sharing, and the healing work that followed, was touching to us all.

On Sunday afternoon, the group with the bus had to leave early to start on their long journey home. Before they left, as Chuck was starting to say goodbye to them, that young man rose and asked for a microphone. This is a transcription of his words:

"My mom and dad drank a lot when I was younger, so I never felt loved. I never knew what love was. I went to a residential school [for "Indians"]. I was constantly beaten for things that I felt I did not do. I was put down in a lot of ways, so again, I never felt loved.

"Because I never felt loved, when I left the residential school, I hit the streets. For four years of my life I slept in back alleys, eating out of garbage cans. I hung out with gang-type people. We fought, we stole, we did everything together–that was where my strength was. But every time I wanted to get ahead, I was put down by these guys I thought were my friends.

"And all my life, all I wanted was to belong somewhere. I wanted a home where there was love, and I've tried a lot of things in my lifetime to fit in, to find acceptance, to find love.

"I never found love. I found very little acceptance. I know these walls everybody has before them. You know all of us here [gesturing to his group], and you know it was hard for me. When I came here I was really, really skeptical you're all full of shit.

"Since that time I've had a change of heart. We started off yesterday with sort of bad feelings. I was part of the group that wanted to leave. But because your wife asked for a chance...on the streets all I wanted was a chance to prove who I was.

"Being a carpenter by trade I know what it is like to tear down walls with hammers, and in order to do it quickly carpenters have to work together as a team. These walls that I'm talking about now are spiritual ones, and we have to get together.

"I now have a glimpse of what love really is. I've looked around. I've been with my wife [who was sitting next to him] for 13 years now, married for 8. We've gone through a lot of hard times ourselves, and one of the reasons I wanted to come was to try and strengthen the relationship that we have.

"I've always needed something in my life. Coming to this workshop has shown me that what I was really looking for has always been around me. Rather than travelling through different towns, travelling through different groups, trying to find the acceptance that I needed.... [Emotion broke his voice and made it difficult to speak.] I'm having a hard time here.

"I always said that I would never allow anyone inside me, because every time I've allowed my feelings to show, I've been hurt; I've been kicked down; I've been put down. I've told a few people that I would never cry, that nobody would know when I was hurting. Nobody would know when I was down, and no one would see me cry. I've cried here this weekend, just feeling the love that is in this room.

"The majority of the people I do not even know, I've never seen before. But there are faces here that remind me of people that I've been with, that I've lived with, that I've shared a common ground with.

"What I'm trying to say is that we have to work together as humans–*forget* nationalities. We have already seen what nationalities can do to each other, everybody trying to put down others' nationalities. I would like to believe that I am just another human.... We all put on a pair of pants in the morning, we all put on socks and shoes, make love in the same way. We all have brothers and sisters and mothers and fathers. Let's all just look at ourselves as humans and just open our hearts and our minds, because what I've had to do this weekend is open my heart and my mind.

"Like I said, I was skeptical, and now I have a different point of view, feeling the love that I have felt in this whole entire room. The streets have never given me that and, well... this is just too hard. [He struggled to be able to speak.]

"I just want to say thank you to every one of you, and especially to you and your wife, Chuck, for showing me through your demonstrations that love is within us, love is around us–we just have to open our hearts and our minds to accept it."

Chuck responded by saying there was one thing that he could do before he left that would really strengthen his relationship with his wife, if he would like to do it; it would not take long. The young man agreed, and Chuck invited him and his wife to come to the center of the room (seating was arranged in a U shape). He placed the young man and himself at one end of the U and the young man's wife near me at the other end.

Then Chuck asked him which two people in this room reminded him of his parents...not necessarily in how they looked but perhaps in how they felt to him.

"I would have to say it is people I am well familiar with. The one person who would play my mom is not here, and that is our chief, Mildred Swan. She talked yesterday. [She had not been in the seminar room this day at all.] And for my father, I would have to say George [the 'cowboy/Indian']."

Then, at that exact moment a loud noise announced the opening of the huge swinging doors, and Mildred burst into the room (Heaven was showing off). She had come in to tell her group that the bus was ready and waiting.

Chuck explained to Mildred that we were doing something to heal a relationship between a husband and wife–to bring it up to a new level of love. Would she and George help? They agreed, and he placed them in the middle of the U.

Chuck then addressed the young man, telling him that what stood between him and his wife was a painful belief that he would always have to be independent, to "go it alone," because his parents had not "been there for him." This had helped him survive on the streets, but now it was preventing closeness with his wife. Part of him was saying, "I do not need her at all," and the rest of him was saying, "I need her a lot." It was as if an invisible wall separated him from his wife.

Chuck explained that when a person complains that their parents did not give them something, it is because the person came into this life to give that very thing to their parents. Yet when children come into the family and that certain thing is missing, rather than provide it themselves, they tend to throw themselves away...just as he had thrown himself away.

The gift he had always wanted to give his parents could still be given to them, through a ritual he could enact with these helpers. He could look them in the eyes, make peace with them, forgive them, and go gather them up in love and grace. Then, because he had supported them, he could bring them to his wife as a support, rather than a block, to their relationship.

Next he could to look into his wife's eyes, and with nothing between them, go to join her. It would take great courage to give up the "survivor" personality in order to have a new level of partnership with her, but it would be what she has always been waiting for. She had never felt loved either. His gift would change that.

I put a song on the sound system, and the young man looked at his "parents," facing his grievances, anger and hurt. He used all of his courage and strength to work through his feelings and find forgiveness. It took the time span of three songs before he could honestly and in truth, walk to the two people standing in the center of the room and embrace them. It was a powerful emotional release for all three of them (as well as for many others in the room), each for their own reasons.

The three then walked arm in arm to the young man's wife, including her in the embrace, breaking through the wall. Soon after, Chuck and I and the whole bus load of people joined them. Then everyone else in the seminar was in the center of the room. They shared their love and made their farewells to the First Nation people. It was a happy group that finally got on that bus and headed for home.

At our next Psychology of Vision International Training in Hawaii, I realized how lucky we all were to enjoy the flavor of being members of the world community...citizens of planet earth with a sense of membership in the human race that was stronger than any political, national or racial identities.

We were a rainbow of genetics and cultures, communicating with each other through five languages, but joined by a powerful bondedness that established with no uncertainty that Heaven is real. I realized, as I looked around the room, that only one generation ago all of our parents had been at war with one another.

How blessed we all were to know and love each other with such lack of separation. Heaven's vision is the answer to every human conflict, fear and need.

...by perceiving light, darkness automatically disappears.
A Course in Miracles, Text, p. 3

THE BOYS
by Mark Wadleigh

During a personal session with Lency I discovered that grace, love, and happiness are a matter of personal choice. I was able to experience, for the first time, the crystal clear and vivid mechanics of the choosing and re-choosing process that was already always taking place deep inside of me.

My problem was that a 10-year-old boy, Adamje, was staying with me for a couple of weeks, while his mother, a dear friend of mine named Tamzon, was out of the country. He is an only child, a truly wonderful boy, and he and I are very close.

In previous years our many visits were happy and carefree. In a week's time, there would typically be one or two five-minute episodes where he got obnoxious and/or I got cranky. This visit, for some reason, it was I who was cranky the whole time. Adamje got on my nerves, he could not seem (to me) to do anything right, and I found myself crabbing away at him like I sometimes remember my dad crabbing away at me when I was 10.

I was feeling the pain of being myself at age 10, and I was also feeling the pain of being an ineffective "parent." I was really disappointed in myself. It was like I was possessed by these different people: myself at age 10, Adamje in the present time, and my dad when I was 10. I really felt split, like I was not myself anymore.

On top of all that, I was also feeling the pain of being with someone I really loved without being able to feel any of the joy or comfort of that love. Instead, I was feeling guilt, pain, remorse, and despair.

150

During Adamje's last two or three days with me I approached Lency and asked her for help. Would she sit with me and help me "feel" through this, because as it was, I was miserable. I was desperate. I was at the end of my rope, and was totally and completely ready to stop having no love. Whatever it took, I was ready for love.

After arranging for Chuck to watch the kids, Lency and I went into the office and faced each other on the couch. I told her my story, pretty much like I just did here, and opened myself up to whatever she would do.

She placed a hand on my chest, and started to feel around. Then she put the other hand on me too, and said she could feel some sadness inside of me. At first I could not feel it. I felt the pressure of my problem pushing down on me from above, and I felt like a failure to be loving towards the boy. There was a hint of desperation, a little guilt, and a sense of speed, of velocity, like traveling down a highway in a scorching gray desert (going nowhere).

Then Lency put her head down and leaned her weight through her hands onto my chest. As she was physically making this contact with me, I felt a tremendous sense of safety. I began to feel a connection with her, a warmth, a companionship, a "looked-afterness." It would be easy to say I felt mothered, but that's not accurate. Rather, I felt that I was loved, and someone competent was on the job. I felt friendship, partnership, and in the presence of an energy that was greater than my mind, great enough to heal me.

Various scenarios of me as a kid came floating up from inside me. The visions were all of the time when I was around the ages of 10 to 13, which were particularly rough years for me.

At times the feelings would be strongest in my chest, at times in my throat. At times they were mostly physical, then emotional, then a blend. Then after a few minutes, my sternum began to burn where her hands touched me. It felt like she was applying a red hot branding iron to me. *Literally.* It was a sharp, scorching sensation that I could feel in my flesh and bones. Yet it felt totally appropriate, and very, *very healing.*

And for clarity, let me say that she was not poking me or pinching me or anything like that. She was actually touching me very gently with her finger tips and sometimes the palms of her hands. That's all. The energy flowing through was the source of the burning.

It was a very satisfying feeling. The word delicious comes up. I felt like I was being healed.

Then Lency asked me if I could feel the love. I felt that something very good was happening, but I did not know if it was *love* proper, so I hemmed and hawed a little, and she said, "See if you can feel yourself being loved. Look for that."

Then I started feeling a rushing, tickling, sparkling energy shooting up my spine. I felt like I was being reamed out (in my spine up through my head), by a giant feather duster. I recognized this as classic kundalini activity, and did not resist it in any way. After 5 or 10 minutes of that, when I could sit upright again, Lency again asked me if I could feel the love.

At first I did not see the point. Just because I could not feel the love—so what? I was in the middle of something powerful and useful!

After she asked me for the fifth or sixth time, "Can you feel yourself being loved? Can you feel the love?" I began to search around inside more closely. Where was this love thing? Meanwhile, problem after problem relating to my situation had been floating up, and we'd been burning through them. Overall, I was feeling good. When I looked "up" for the love, all I could feel was the burn process.

Then I remembered a time a few months before when I had a clear experience of how Lency saw me. Her version of who I am is the most beautiful person. Not in a flashy, "fashion" way, but rather in a sweet, natural, loving and divine way. It was very touching to think that somebody held me in this clarity, in this high esteem, even when I saw myself as a fat, crabby old loser.

Well anyway, during the session with Lency I'm describing here, I began to get frustrated because I could not find love anywhere. Then a funny thought popped into my head: look once again at that vision of myself that Lency had.

So I did. It was almost like cheating, it was so easy. I instantly felt love, and surprise. For a micro-second I was surprised that the love was there. Then I knew that I always knew the love was there, but that I had erected this big gray barrier to feeling it. That too was surprising. It was somewhat vague, but I did have the certain remembrance of this whole scenario of hiding love from myself.

As soon as the feeling of love came, another feeling rose up from underneath me, a feeling of worry, unease, and dread. I told Lency, "Yes, I feel the love, but something else needs to be handled first. I have to burn through something else first."

Lency said, "Let's try an experiment. Let's not burn through it. Let's just say we can choose to feel the love right now, without having to go through anything. Would you be willing to try that?"

I said I would, and she reminded me to leave the problem feeling alone. Do not deny it, or move it, or anything. Just put my awareness on love and leave it there.

This worked, but it was the oddest thing. And herein lies the crux, for me anyway, of choice. The feeling of wrongness, the feeling of a problem being present, did not negate the feeling of love, it merely denied it for me at this time. It was as if accompanying the feeling was a verbal instruction that said, "Because this feeling (the problem) is larger now, it commands the floor. You must choose it."

The interpretation of what the feeling meant was so strong that I did not even question it, let alone defy it. In fact, one of the interesting things about the experience was the sudden realization that this interpretation had been attached to problem feelings all of my life, and was functioning as a way for me to choose dread and postpone happiness. What was amazing was that I never consciously knew I had that interpretation going on.

Following Lency's instructions was a matter of moving my awareness, my attention, from the problem feeling to the sight of me seen through loving eyes, which evoked the feeling of love and being loved. While I did that the interpretation inside me was screaming at the top of its lungs, "Don't! You can't! It won't work! It won't work!"

Also present in the resistance was a feeling of mild shock, like a tradition was being violated, as if a part of me was saying, "What? Do it differently? But we've always done it this way!" Who wants to defy tradition?

I did it anyway! The feeling of love was there, and in a micro-second was replaced by a feeling of dread. Then, without fighting the dread or analyzing it or doing anything with it, I merely moved my attention over to the feeling of being loved.

Shifting my attention was like shifting car headlights. I knew it could not work, because that yucky dread feeling inside told me it could not. It told me I was not lovable yet, that I had to handle this other thing first. I did not argue the point, I just moved those "headlights" of my attention over to being loved *anyway.*

It is important to note that I did not try to negate the dread, or to change it. I just moved my attention. I did not try to subtract anything. I added the bigger truth that, in spite of everything: *I was loved right now and always have been and always will be.* In the face of that shift of attention, which was maintained by my intention that it be maintained, the dread feeling went away, like air from a deflated balloon. It went quickly, in a matter of seconds.

After the first problem dissolved in the face of my feeling loved, the second problem came and went, then the third, then the fourth. Each one went away faster and faster, and the focus on love was easier and easier. A feeling of bliss, joy, and ecstasy started to build in me, and got quite strong. My whole life looked unreal; only love was real.

It was as if the question were asked: What if all your bad feelings were untrue? What if you just made them up? And what if all you had to do to heal them was to allow them to be, and to choose happiness and love? Would I be willing to at least try that on as an experiment?

I did, and it worked. All I had to do was be willing to be wrong about having to be miserable. I only had to be willing to be wrong about not deserving love. I only had to make room for it. And I did that by remembering it.

I genuinely saw that love is not anything to wait for. It cannot be earned. It just is, and right now, forever. All I had to do was see how I had been choosing something else instead of love, decide instead to choose love, and then just do it! It is easy!

After our session together, the tension I had experienced with my young ward evaporated. Adamje seemed happier, more at ease, and more playful. What had annoyed me before had either changed, vanished, or maybe I was just seeing it differently. Whatever the reason, I was able to enjoy his childlike energy, enthusiasm, and innocence, and really appreciate him. Our last few days together were great!

You have the ability to heal others through your love, if only you can find it. You are needed on the earth, Sweetheart, and many await you.

Miracles are teaching devices for demonstrating it is as blessed to give as to receive. They simultaneously increase the strength of the giver and supply strength to the receiver.

A Course in Miracles, Text, p. 2

CHOOSE ONLY LOVE

A great many people throughout history have had experiences of the love we have examined in this book. It seems the most common access to the experience of great love comes from pre-death visions (like those of little Elijah), or near-death experiences (mystical experiences that happen to people who almost die).

In his 1990 book, *Closer to the Light: Learning from the Near-Death Experiences of Children,* Dr. Melvin Morse (a pediatrician and leader in the field of near-death research), cites that a poll conducted in 1982 by the George Gallup organization found an estimated eight million near-death experiences in the United States.

In the classic near-death episode, the subject experiences tremendous love and caring emanating from a brilliant Light, or a Being of Light. Some people call him "God," "Allah," "Jesus," an "Angel," or simply "The Man." My favorite story of a near-death experience was written by psychiatrist George G. Ritchie, in the book he wrote in 1978, *Return From Tomorrow.* As a 20-year-old U.S. Army private going through basic training in 1943, Ritchie "died" of pneumonia. At the hospital, his body was covered with a sheet, ready to be taken to the morgue.

Finding himself standing beside his own body, Ritchie encountered a "Man made out of Light," whom he recognized as Jesus. With certainty, he knew that this Man loved him with an astonishing love. A love beyond his wildest imagining. A love that knew all of the unlovable things about him, and accepted him and loved him just the same.

Ritchie then was shown every single episode of his whole life, all seeming to take place at the same moment. At the end, the Man asked, "What have you done with your life to show Me?"

Ritchie realized that the question had to do with love. How much have you loved with your life? Have you loved others as I am loving you? Totally? Unconditionally?

Ritchie thought, indignantly, "Why hadn't I known love like this was possible? Someone should have told me! A fine time to discover what life was all about–like coming to a final exam and discovering you were going to be tested on a subject you had never studied! If this was the point of everything, why hadn't someone told me?"

The Being then showed him fascinating glimpses of life after death before returning him to his body. Ritchie was terribly distressed to return to this life, wondering how he could live without the presence of the love.

After this encounter, as a World War II medic in Europe, Ritchie experienced a desire to die, even wondering if he had been brought back to life as a punishment. Then one day he encountered a wounded officer with a familiar and beautiful look in his eyes.

Not recognizing at first what it was that so attracted him to this man, he finally realized that the look reminded him of the look of love that he had seen coming from the Man of Light. He could see "Christ" looking out at him through the wounded officer's eyes.

He realized that the lonesomeness and alienation which he had been feeling for the year since his near-death experience was all about his longing to be back in the presence of the Being's love. He now understood that he could experience that love in the eyes of the people he encountered every day.

When the war in Europe ended in May, 1945, Ritchie's unit provided medical help to newly liberated prisoners at a concentration camp near Wuppertal, Germany. The experience was horrifying. Conditions had been so desperate that men continued to die by the score every day, despite the U.S. Army's frantic provisions of food and medical care.

When the despair became too great to handle, Ritchie walked from one end of the camp to the other, looking into men's faces until he saw, looking back at him, the eyes of Christ. That was how he met a Polish Jew nick-named "Wild Bill" by the Americans because of his long drooping handlebar mustache. He had been one of the prisoners, but obviously not for long: his posture was erect, his eyes were bright, his health was radiant. He worked up to 16 hours a day to help the Americans, but showed no sign of fatigue.

Speaking six languages, Wild Bill proved invaluable in the process of identifying and relocating the inmates, as well as arbitrating in quarrels between inmates of different nationalities, and even counseling forgiveness towards the Germans. (It was not uncommon in other camps for the former prisoners to grab guns, run to the nearest village and shoot the first German they saw.)

You can imagine Ritchie's great surprise at learning that Wild Bill had actually been an inmate at that concentration camp for six years, performing the same work, eating the same starvation diet and exposed to the same diseases that had killed thousands of other men. Ritchie wondered what could have saved his life.

One day Wild Bill told Ritchie what it was that made him so different. It all came from a choice he had made years before.

Wild Bill had lived with his wife and five children in the Jewish ghetto in Warsaw. The Nazis came and forced everyone out of their houses, lined them up against the wall, and shot them with machine guns.

Wild Bill's family was murdered in front of his eyes, but the soldiers ignored his plea to be killed alongside them. Because of his ability to speak German, his life was spared and he was put in a work group.

The obvious and usual response would have been for Wild Bill to hate the soldiers; for most people it would be the automatic reaction. Certainly no one would have faulted Wild Bill for doing so. Instead, a miracle occurred. Wild Bill was shown, in this most dire and compelling of circumstances, that indeed he had a *choice* in the matter.

He could hate the soldiers who had done this, thereby committing himself to a life of hate and a future that would be nothing but a product of hate; or, he could choose love, and the life that would be love's outcome.

Wild Bill chose love, deciding that, for the rest of his life–however long or short it might be–he would love every single person with whom he came into contact. He started with those Nazi soldiers.

Love had kept him strong and well. Love had given him life.

Could you venture to live your life through your open heart? You have lived too long with it closed, withdrawn from the world. You have contracted from the experiences life provides. You have become afraid of life, and afraid of other people. You have made yourself small in hopes that you will slip through life without attracting more pain.

Yet the smaller your heart becomes, the more painful life is...you are less and less able to receive the one thing that makes life worth living.

Without an open heart, love passes you by, and you cannot taste Heaven's grace. Any experience may be seen in beauty if it is witnessed through an open heart.

Miracles are examples of right thinking, aligning your perceptions with
truth as God created it.
A Course in Miracles, Text, p. 3

HAPPINESS

For some time I had known that I could feel love and
happiness anytime I wanted. I knew exactly where the door
that opened to peacefulness, comfort and joy was located in
my heart.

I did spend some time with that door open. Always when
I joined with others, always when something nice happened
or I was swept away by the beauty of the Islands.

Yet, how could I explain all the times in between? The
times when I could so easily choose happiness but did not
want to, or felt I just could not. I would not feel happy, as
if to feel happiness would mean I would lose my chance to
take vengeance on life.

This part of me that would not choose happiness felt like
a sour and surly teenager who would not allow her parents
the pleasure of seeing her smile. My resentment was more
important to me than happiness. Even though I had every
reason to be happy, I just could not seem to muster the
willingness to take that step.

While this dilemma was swimming around in my mind,
Chuck, the kids, and I went to the neighbor island of Hawaii
for a 22-day segment of our International Training. We
stayed at an incredible resort hotel built on acres of gorgeous
lagoons, brilliant pools, tumbling waterfalls, pristine tropical
gardens, picturesque coconut palm groves, and dramatic
views of the ocean beating against the black lava shore.

Somehow, even water slides, swims with dolphins, and
organized activities with other kids had not made my children

happy. At least not during the time they spent with me. When we were together they squabbled and competed for my attention. If one wanted to take the train ride to our room, the other claimed to *hate* train rides and only wanted to ride the boat back. They seemed to be constantly incurring "owies" and "boo-boos" that demanded serious kissing and attention.

At the end of the first week I was feeling miserable whenever I was with them. I felt a depression that accused me of hating motherhood and of not liking my children, and that whispered to me that I was caught in this trap of torture for life.

Finally I had a talk with the kids. I explained how rough it was for me to be with them when they fussed so much. I explained that it may not seem like they had the power to choose whether they feel happy or unhappy, because it often looks like it is the things that happen that cause their feelings. The truth is that the responsibility for their happiness is theirs, and that at any moment they could choose to be happy.

Initially, I felt relief after "straightening them out." After a while I realized I was not feeling good at all. Actually, if I really looked at it, I would recognize that I felt guilty for attacking them.

It was actually ridiculous for me to come down so hard on my children rather than see how perfectly they were reflecting my own mind. I was chastising them for not taking the step that I had not been willing to take myself. I had admonished them for not choosing to feel happiness that I had been too immature to allow into my own heart. I saw that their unhappiness, and mine, were the same.

I had finally found the motivation that would help me take that step! I knew that choosing happiness for myself would be the same as choosing it for them. Making that choice became much easier. I simply chose.

Poof! My bad attitude was gone. I was thrilled by a tremendous tenderness and sense of devotion to my children! I felt innocent and felt like a good and loving mother. And the door was open–at least a crack–to the warm stream of happiness and love.

I watched my mental conversation for thoughts of attack (attack I perceived as coming towards me as well as attack that was going from me to others). I knew that my own sense of innocence and happiness depended on my willingness to give up those thoughts, and live without judgement.

What I experienced when I was with the children next was a happy surprise. They were both so totally at peace that they treated each other and me with exquisite affection, appreciation, and honor. Their sweetness and fine, rich beauty was so delicious that our time together was filled with grace and joy. We found ourselves back in the Garden.

To choose happiness and love is to stretch yourself to become bigger, to be less defended, to feel closer to other people, to be more generous, to reach for your center, to receive from your Source. It is to feel safety, to see beauty, to walk in grace. It is to choose life.

To move away from life is to choose love's opposite. It is to nurse your wounds, to feel righteous, to not care, to separate yourself from others, to dramatize your suffering, to fight, to compete, to close your heart. It is to feel pain, sadness, and fear. It is to choose death.

Life is a continuous challenge which confronts us with only one question over and over again in every instant: Now, in this moment, will you choose to feel happiness and love, or will you choose to feel pain and fear? Will you shine the light of your heart and mind into the darkness, or will you hold it back?

Countless times a day we are faced with the choice: will I respond to a challenge with maturity, putting the best construction on everything, extending myself, opening my heart to the point of experiencing contact and love? Or will I react with indulgence, separating myself further, feasting on the pleasure of feeling hurt and righteous?

Even though immaturity reaps painful results, it is extremely difficult to pass up its temptations. It feels so good to over-react, to even the score, to attack back, and to relive grievances.

It takes great wisdom to make the choice for life, and great practice to make the choice constantly. Yet it is only in this choice, this choosing of our hearts, that we can MAKE WAY FOR LOVE.

As the children taught, Sweetheart, love is what is important in life. Love is everything.

It is pouring out to you in every moment. All you need do is receive it. All you need do is attend to it, and it will beautify your world in every way.

Your time in this life is precious. The purpose of time is to find the love. Look for it everywhere. Look for the love in every face you see, to learn of your own innocence and beauty, and to lead you back to the Garden.

You are wholly lovable, Sweetheart, and wholly loved. Heaven awaits...follow your heart, and find your way Home!

Lency Spezzano, M.S.

Lency Spezzano lives in the country on the island of Oahu, Hawaii with her husband Chuck and their two children. She is a director of Spezzano and Associates, Ltd., a company which conducts lectures and seminars on the Psychology of Vision® worldwide.

BOOKS, TAPES and INFORMATION

To order any materials by either Lency or Chuck Spezzano, or to inquire about their lectures and seminars:

U.S.A.　(Monday to Friday, 8:00am-4:30pm, Hawaii Standard Time)

Spezzano and Associates
47-416 Waihee Place　　　　Tel: (808) 239-4502
Kaneohe, HI 96744　　　　　Fax: (808) 239-5424

To order *Make Way For Love,* only, please call
(800) 247-6553

CANADA　(Business hours, Vancouver, B.C., Pacific Time)

Tel: (604) 298-6766
Fax: (604) 298-6755

UNITED KINGDOM

Psychology of Vision Partnership, UK
Vision Center
PO Box 7
Leatherhead, Surrey KT23 4YF
England